THE GERMAN HANDBOOK

A Practical Grammar Guide

PAUL WEBSTER

CAMBRIDGE
UNIVERSITY PRESS

using the **Handbook**

If you are in the first years of learning German, the *German Handbook* is intended for you. From this book, you can find out from scratch how the language works, and how to use it accurately when you are speaking or writing everyday German. The essentials are – I hope – clearly explained, with small points and exceptions included where necessary and useful, but this is not an exhaustive grammar summary. It does, however, contain all you need to know up to at least GCSE (and equivalent) level. PAUL WEBSTER

Abbreviations used

acc.	accusative	m.	masculine	
adj.	adjective	neut.	neuter	
dat.	dative	nom.	nominative	
f.	feminine	pl.	plural	
gen.	genitive	sing.	singular	
inf.	infinitive	usw.	und so weiter (= etc.)	
		z.B.	zum Beispiel (= e.g.)	

Symbols used

* *   verb which takes **sein** (see 10.22)
* 🔑   key material (the most basic, important material)
* !   points on which errors are very common
* •   essential verbs on the Verb list

components of the course

SCHWARZ ■ ROT ■ GOLD

(The Course Book)   0 521 27883 X

Twenty Themen – wide variety of materials and approaches – an emphasis on communicative skills combined with work on structures – practice in all four language skills in each Thema – an emphasis on authenticity – carefully cross-referenced for use with **The German Handbook.**

SCHWARZ ■ ROT ■ GOLD

The German Handbook   0 521 27882 1

Practical, readable reference book for all learners in their first years of German – all the German grammar needed up to GCSE level explained simply and with a minimum of technical terms.

SCHWARZ ■ ROT ■ GOLD

Set of 3 Cassettes   0 521 26248 8

Dialogues from the course book – scripted and unscripted listening comprehension material.

SCHWARZ ■ ROT ■ GOLD

Teacher's Edition   0 521 27884 0

The course book – plus teaching notes – plus tapescript – plus answers – plus reproduction masters for revision, and for help with writing.

PUBLISHED BY THE PRESS SYNDICATE OF THE UNIVERSITY OF CAMBRIDGE
The Pitt Building, Trumpington Street, Cambridge CB2 1RP, United Kingdom

CAMBRIDGE UNIVERSITY PRESS
The Edinburgh Building, Cambridge CB2 2RU, United Kingdom
40 West 20th Street, New York, NY 10011–4211, USA
10 Stamford Road, Oakleigh, Melbourne 3166, Australia

First published 1987
Fourteenth printing 1997

Printed in the United Kingdom at the University Press, Cambridge

A catalogue record for this book is available from the British Library

ISBN 0 521 27882 1 paperback

Author's acknowledgement

I would like to thank Leslie Russon for the extreme care with which he commented on my manuscript. Any imperfections and misjudgements that remain are entirely mine.

Library of Congress cataloguing in publication data
Webster, Paul, 1952–
  Schwarz Rot Gold
  1. German language – Grammar – 1950 –
  2. German language – Text-books for foreign speakers–
  English. I. Title.
  PF3112.W354 1987   438.2'421   86–20735

contents

nouns

1.1 ● What is a noun?

A noun is a word which names a thing, a person, a concept or anything else!

> z.B.   der **Bus**, der **Mann**, die **Freundschaft**, das **Land**, der **Tag**

Capital letters
All true nouns in German have a capital letter: der **B**us, der **M**ann, etc.

1.2 ● The three genders

All German nouns belong to one of three large groups. These are known as the three genders – masculine, feminine and neuter. The markers and adjective forms used with each noun depend on which gender the noun belongs to; markers and adjectives are explained in section 2. The words for people, things and concepts can belong to any of the three genders – there is not much logic about it. For example, the words for *knife*, *fork* and *spoon* each belong to a different gender:

spoon	**der** Löffel (m.)	
fork	**die** Gabel (f.)	
knife	**das** Messer (n.)	

The word for *person* is feminine (**die** Person), even when it refers to a man, and the word for *girl* (**das** Mädchen) is neuter! The only way to cope with this is to regard the word for *the* (**der**, **die** or **das**) as part of each noun and learn it with the noun, so do not think of the word for *bus* as **Bus**, but as **der Bus**.

Although the genders are not logical, the following notes will help.

(a) Masculine
Far more nouns are in the masculine than in either of the other genders. The following are masculine:

days	z.B.	**der** Sonntag
months	z.B.	**der** Mai
seasons	z.B.	**der** Winter
male persons	z.B.	**der** Mann, **der** Onkel, **der** Taxifahrer
makes of car	z.B.	**der** Porsche, **der** VW-Golf (BUT: **das** Auto)

many short nouns formed by removing **-en** from infinitives:

	z.B.	**der** Schlaf	*sleep*
		der Anfang	*start*
		der Schrei	*scream*

most nouns ending in **-el** or **-er**:

> z.B.   **der** Apfel,   **der** Computer

(b) Feminine

female persons   z.B. **die** Frau,   **die** Schwester
(UNLESS the noun ends in **-chen** or **-lein**: **das** Mädchen, **das** Fräulein)

numbers   z.B. Ich habe **eine** Eins geschrieben.
                               I got a grade one.

nouns with these endings:

-ei	die Bäckerei	*bakery*
-ie	die Drogerie	*chemists*
-ung	die Zeitung	*newspaper*
-heit	die Krankheit	*illness*
-keit	die Höflichkeit	*politeness*
-tion	die Information	*information*
-schaft	die Landschaft	*landscape*

most words ending in **-e**:

              z.B.   **die** Blume   *flower*
(BUT there are also many masculine nouns ending in **-e**: **der** Löwe *lion*)

(c) Neuter

infinitives used as nouns:

              z.B.   **das** Schwimmen   *swimming*

words ending in **-chen** or **-lein**. These words usually refer to something small or young:

              z.B.   **das** Mädchen   *girl*
                      das Türchen   *little door*
                      das Kindlein   *little child*

words ending in **-o**, **-um** or **-ment**:

              z.B.   **das** Radio, **das** Museum, **das** Experiment

!   *der See* or *die See*?

      der See   *lake*
      die See   *sea* (=das Meer)

Both words have the plural **Seen** – pronounced **See-en**.

1.3 • Compound nouns

German often puts two or more words together to make a new noun (known in grammar as a compound noun):

      z.B. groß + der Vater ⟶ der Großvater *grandfather*

The gender of a compound noun is decided by the noun at the end of it:

      z.B. das Auto + die Fabrik ⟶ **die** Autofabrik *car factory*

1.4 ● **Plurals**

German has a variety of ways of making nouns plural. When you learn a noun, it is useful to learn not only its gender but also its plural. Dictionaries and vocabularies usually show how to form the plural in a shortened form, e.g. das Buch (¨er). This means that the plural is Bücher. Umlaut (¨) can be added to **a, o, u** and **au** (which becomes **äu**). In a compound word, it is the last main vowel which is affected, e.g. der Großvater (¨) has the plural Großväter. The following notes will give you some help with plurals.

(a) Masculine plurals

The most usual plural is **-e**, with Umlaut added if possible:

z.B. der Tisch (**-e**), der Schrank (**¨e**)

EXCEPTIONS: der Tag (**-e**), der Hund (**-e**), der Arm (**-e**), der Schuh (**-e**), der Punkt (**-e**) and some others do not add the expected Umlaut.

Masculine nouns ending in **-el, -en, -er** never add an ending in the plural, but some of them add Umlaut:

z.B. der Wagen (**-**), der Fahrer (**-**) BUT der Laden (**¨**) and der Apfel (**¨**)

(b) Feminine plurals

The most usual plural is **-n** or **-en**:
z.B. die Lampe (**-n**), die Frau (**-en**)

Words ending in **-in** add **-nen**:
z.B. die Freundin (**-nen**)

Most feminine nouns ending in **-el** or **-er** add **-n** for the plural:

z.B. die Tafel (**-n**), die Schwester (**-n**)

EXCEPTIONS: die Mutter (**¨**), die Tochter (**¨**)

A few common feminine nouns add **¨e**:

z.B. die Hand (**¨e**), die Wand (**¨e**), die Stadt (**¨e**), die Nacht (**¨e**), die Maus (**¨e**), die Kuh (**¨e**)

(c) Neuter plurals

Many common neuter nouns add **-e**. There is no Umlaut added:

z.B. das Haar (**-e**), das Spiel (**-e**), das Zelt (**-e**)

Many other neuter nouns add **-er** with Umlaut if possible:

z.B. das Kleid (**-er**), das Buch (**¨er**)

Note these common neuter nouns, which unexpectedly have the plural **-n/-en**: das Auge (**-n**), das Ohr (**-en**), das Hemd (**-en**), das Bett (**-en**), das Ende (**-n**)

⚠ (d) Plural in English, but singular in German

die Hose	*pair of trousers*	die Schere	*pair of scissors*
die Brille	*pair of glasses*	die Treppe	*(flight of) stairs*

7

! **(e) Plural verb in English, but singular verb in German**

There are some singular English nouns which we often use with a plural verb, such as *family* and *police*. These must have a singular verb in German.

z.B. Die Familie Schmidt **macht** heute ein Picknick.
The Schmidt family **are going** on a picnic today.

Die Polizei **hat** den Dieb verhaftet.
The police **have** arrested the thief.

! **(f) Plural in German, but singular in English**

die Möbel (pl.) *(pieces of) furniture*
die Lebensmittel (pl.) *food (i.e. groceries)*

1.5 ● Other noun endings

In the *genitive singular* of masculine and neuter nouns, **-s** or **-es** is added. Usually, **-es** is added to short words and **-s** to longer words, but this is not a strict rule (see 3.9).

z.B. Das ist ein Foto **meines Sohn(e)s.**
This is a photo of my son.
This rule does not apply to weak nouns (see 1.6 below).

In the *dative plural*, **-n** is added to the noun plural, unless this already ends in **-n**, or in **-s**:

z.B. den Kinder**n**, den Frau**en**, den Baby**s**

1.6 ● Weak nouns

These nouns are a small group of masculine words which end in **-n** or **-en** in all their forms except for the nominative singular.

z.B. der Junge *boy*

	sing.	pl.
nom.	der Jung**e**	die Jung**en**
acc.	den Jung**en**	die Jung**en**
gen.	des Jung**en** [no s]	der Jung**en**
dat.	dem Jung**en**	den Jung**en**

In vocabulary lists, this is shown in the following way: **der Junge (-n, -n)**, to show that there is **n** added in the singular as well as in the plural. Here is a list of the common weak nouns you will meet:

der Mensch (-en, -en) *person, human being*

der Neffe (-n, -n) *nephew*

der Student (-en, -en) *student*

der Polizist (-en,-en) *policeman*

der Tourist (-en, -en) *tourist*

der Journalist (-en, -en) *journalist*

der Matrose (-n, -n) *sailor*

der Soldat (-en, -en) *soldier*

der Pilot (-en, -en) *pilot*

der Kunde (-n, -n) *customer*

der Bauer (-n, -n) *farmer*

der Nachbar (-n, -n) *neighbour*

der Ire (-n, -n) *Irishman*

8

der Franzose (-n, -n) *Frenchman*
der Russe (-en, -en) *Russian*
der Schotte (-n, -n) *Scot*

der Name (-n, -n) *name*
(this word has an irregular
genitive: des Namen**s**)

| ! |

Herr (meaning *Mr* or *gentleman*) adds **-n** in the singular but **-en** in the plural.

z.B. Herr Müller ist krank. (nom.)
Herr Müller is ill.

Hast du Herr**n** Schmidt gesehen? (acc.)
Have you seen Herr Schmidt?

Das ist Herr**n** Brauns Auto. (gen.)
That's Herr Braun's car.

Kann ich mit Herr**n** Grün sprechen? (dat.)
Can I speak to Herr Grün?

Die beiden Herr**en** sind da. (nom. pl.)
The two gentlemen are here.

1.7 ● Adjectival nouns

These are nouns which have endings as if they were adjectives – the word **Mann** or **Frau** is understood:

der deutsche Mann ⟶ der Deutsch**e**
ein deutsch**er** Mann ⟶ ein Deutsch**er**
eine deutsche Frau ⟶ eine Deutsch**e**

(For the details of the possible adjective endings, see section 2.) **Note** that these nouns begin with a capital letter, like other nouns. The other adjectival nouns you are likely to meet are:

der Verwandte *relative*
der Bekannte *acquaintance, friend*
der Beamte *official, civil servant*

| ! |

Note that **beide** and **andere** have similar endings but they do not have capital letters.

These examples show them in use:

z.B. Jens und Renate gehen **beide** ins Kino.
Jens and Renate are **both** going to the cinema.

Die beiden gehen ins Kino.
The two of them are going to the cinema.

Jutta blieb zu Hause. **Die anderen** gingen in die Disko.
Jutta stayed at home. **The others** went to the disco.

markers
adjectives
adverbs

2

2.1 ● What is a marker?

Nouns do not usually stand alone; they are usually 'introduced' by words such as **der**, **ein**, **mein**, **dieser**. In this book such words are called 'markers' – you can think of them as 'marking out' the nouns. There is a fixed number of them, and they are all given in this section together with their own special endings systems. They often introduce adjectives as well. This table shows all three in action:

marker	adjective	noun
der	neue	Supermarkt
eine	alte	Dame
diese	furchtbare	Grammatik
mein		Opa
	gute	Freunde

Note that there need not always be both a marker and an adjective.

2.2 ● What is an adjective?

Adjectives are words that describe.

> z.B.   Jan ist **intelligent**.
>
> Jan ist ein **intelligenter** Junge.

In the first example, the adjective **intelligent** stands alone (not directly in front of the noun it describes). In German, adjectives which stand alone have no endings. In the second example, the adjective directly describes the noun **Junge**. When an adjective is in this position in German, it must have an adjective ending.

2.3 • The three systems for markers and adjectives

German has three systems of endings for markers and adjectives. This means three tables to learn! It is not quite as complicated as it seems at first, because many of the endings are the same in the different tables. These examples show the three types:

(a) *der/die/das* system

> **Das Postamt** ist nicht weit von hier.
>
> **Das neue Postamt** ist nicht weit von hier.
>
> **Dieser Pullover kostet** nur 20 Mark.
> (For details, see 2.4 and 2.5.)

(b) *ein/eine/ein* system

> **Eine Langspielplatte** kostet 25 Mark.
>
> **Eine gute Langspielplatte** kostet 25 Mark.
>
> **Meine Katze** heißt Mitzi.
>
> **Unser neues Haus** hat drei Schlafzimmer.
> (For details, see 2.6 and 2.7.)

(c) 'no marker' system

> **Viele Schüler** lernen Deutsch.
>
> **Viele englische Schüler** lernen Deutsch.
> (For details, see 2.8.)

2.4 • The *der/die/das* system

These tables show the endings used on markers (and adjectives if used) for the **der/die/das** system. The tables show the four cases (for explanation of cases, see section 3) and the three genders, in both singular and plural.

Singular

	m.	f.	neut.
nom.	**der** gute Mann	**die** gute Frau	**das** gute Kind
acc.	**den** guten Mann	**die** gute Frau	**das** gute Kind
gen.	**des** guten Mannes	**der** guten Frau	**des** guten Kindes
dat.	**dem** guten Mann	**der** guten Frau	**dem** guten Kind

Plural

In the plural, the three genders have identical endings:

nom.	**die** gut**en** Männer/Frauen/Kinder
acc.	**die** gut**en** Männer/Frauen/Kinder
gen.	**der** gut**en** Männer/Frauen/Kinder
dat.	**den** gut**en** Männer**n**/Frauen/Kinder**n**

Note that there is a variety of marker forms (e.g. **der, die, das, den**), but only two adjective endings: **-e** and **-en**. The toothbrush-shaped line in the singular table divides these: **-e** above the line and **-en** everywhere below it, including all of the plural.

2.5 ● **The other markers of the *der/die/das* type**

There are a few other markers which follow the same pattern as **der/die/das** and which are followed by the same system of adjective endings. The most common is **dieser** (*this*):

Singular

	m.	f.	neut.
nom.	dieser	diese	dieses
acc.	diesen	diese	dieses
gen.	dieses	dieser	dieses
dat.	diesem	dieser	diesem

Plural

nom.	diese
acc.	diese
gen.	dieser
dat.	diesen

NOTE that the endings for **dieser** closely resemble **der/die/das**. The only difference is that the neuter nominative and accusative has **-es** (dies**es**), where the **der/die/das** table has **das**.

Other markers of this type are: jeder/jede/jedes   *each, every*

welcher?/welche?/welches?   *which?*

Less common: jener/jene/jenes   *that* (not very common, because **der/die/das** are mostly used for the meaning *that*)

mancher/manche/manches   *many a, some*

2.6 ● The *ein/eine/ein* system

This table shows the endings used on markers (and adjectives if used) for the **ein/eine/ein** system. The table shows the four cases (for explanation of cases, see section 3) and the three genders, in both singular and plural.

Singular

	m.	f.	neut.
nom.	**ein** gut**er** Mann	**eine** gut**e** Frau	**ein** gut**es** Kind
acc.	**einen** gut**en** Mann	**eine** gut**e** Frau	**ein** gut**es** Kind
gen.	**eines** gut**en** Mannes	**einer** gut**en** Frau	**eines** gut**en** Kindes
dat.	**einem** gut**en** Mann	**einer** gut**en** Frau	**einem** gut**en** Kind

Plural

In the plural, the three genders have identical endings. 'A' is not possible in the plural, so the table uses another marker of the same type – **kein**:

nom.	**keine** gut**en** Männer/Frauen/Kinder
acc.	**keine** gut**en** Männer/Frauen/Kinder
gen.	**keiner** gut**en** Männer/Frauen/Kinder
dat.	**keinen** gut**en** Männern/Frauen/Kindern

NOTE that this system is different from the **der/die/das** system only above the toothbrush-shaped line. Below the line, both marker and adjective have the same endings as on the **der/die/das** table. It is only above the line that the two marker systems differ.

2.7 ● The other markers of the *ein/eine/ein* type

Several other markers follow exactly the same pattern as **ein/eine/ein**. These are the possessives and **kein**:

mein	*my*
dein	*your* (corresponds to **du**, see 4.3)
sein	*his, its*
ihr	*her, its*
sein	*its*
unser	*our*
euer	*your* (corresponds to **ihr**, see 4.3)
Ihr	*your* (corresponds to **Sie**, see 4.3)
ihr	*their*
kein	*not a, no*

z.B. **Meine neue Hose** ist blau.
My new trousers are blue.

Das ist **unser neues Auto.**
That's **our new car.**

Karin geht mit **ihrem Freund** aus.
Karin is going out with **her boyfriend.**

NOTE that **kein** must be used instead of „nicht ein":

z.B. Das ist **kein** Kuli (*not* „nicht ein Kuli"), das ist ein Füller.
That is**n't a** ball-point, it's a fountain pen.

(See also 9.12.)

2.8 • The 'no marker' system

Sometimes, nouns and adjectives are used without any marker. In this situation, German basically gives the adjective or adjectives the endings that a marker would have had, if it had been used.

z.B. Vie**le** jung**e** Engländer lernen Deutsch.

NOTE that **viele** is not a marker. In this example we simply have two adjectives (**viele** and **junge**) with a noun (**Engländer**). The 'no marker' system is rare in the singular, so the table below shows only the plural:

nom.	**viele gute** Bücher
acc.	**viele gute** Bücher
gen.	**vieler guter** Bücher
dat.	**vielen guten** Bücher**n**

Apart from **viele**, other adjectives often used in this way are **einige** (*some*), and **wenige** (*few*). The 'no marker' endings are also needed after *numbers* (**zwei** neu**e** Bücher, etc.), **mehr** (*more*) and **weniger** (*fewer*).

2.9 • Adjectives: endings difficulties in the plural. *-e* or *-en*?

If there is *any marker*, the adjective ending is **-en**:

z.B. die
meine
unsere ⎤ neu**en** Schuhe
diese
keine

NOTE that **alle** and **beide** are used like this too:

alle
beide ⎤ neu**en** Schuhe

14

Only when there is *no marker* is the adjective ending **-e**.

z.B. einige ⎤
      viele   ⎥
      wenige ⎥—neu**e** Schuhe
      mehr   ⎥
      weniger ⎥
      zwei   ⎦

! **2.10 ● How to express 'some' and 'any'**

In German there is usually no need for the equivalent of the English words *some* and *any*.

z.B. Haben Sie Brot da?
      Have you **any** bread?

      Ich will Wurst kaufen.
      I want to buy **some** sausage.

      Ich habe Eier gekauft.
      I bought **some** eggs.

When there is a need (see 4.12), **etwas** is used in the singular, and **einige** is used in the plural.

      Er hat **etwas** Brot gegessen.
      He ate **some** (= a bit of) bread.

      Er hat **einige** Kekse gegessen.
      He ate **some** (= a few) biscuits.

NOTE also:

irgendwo   *somewhere, anywhere*

jemand   *someone, somebody, anyone, anybody*

etwas   *something* (in conversation often shortened to **was**)

irgendwie   *somehow*

manchmal   *sometimes*

irgendwann   *sometime*

15

2.11 ● **'the same': *derselbe* and *der gleiche***

derselbe means literally *the same* person or thing:

z.B. Jochen und Hans gehen in **dieselbe** Schule.
Jochen and Hans go to the same school.

der gleiche means a *similar* person or thing:

z.B. Jochen und Hans tragen **den gleichen** Pullover.
Jochen and Hans are wearing the same pullover. (i.e. two identical ones!)

With both expressions, normal marker and adjective endings are needed. **der gleiche** is written as two words; **derselbe** is written as one word, BUT NOTE these alternatives – both are correct:

z.B. Petra und Helga arbeiten **in demselben** Kaufhaus.

OR Petra und Helga arbeiten **im selben** Kaufhaus.

Petra and Helga work in the same department store.

In the second sentence the **der/die/das** part of **derselbe** is combined with the preposition.

2.12 ● **Invariables**

Unlike the adjectives discussed so far, the following words, even though they play a describing role, are invariable – that means they do not vary their endings. These are the common ones:

mehr *more*

weniger *less, fewer*

genug *enough*

ein paar *a few*

z.B. Dieter hat **mehr** Geld als ich.
Dieter has more money than I have.

Ich habe **weniger** Geld als er.
I have less money than he has.

Bekommst du **genug** Taschengeld?
Do you get enough pocket-money?

Ich gehe mit **ein paar** Freunden aus.
I'm going out with a few friends.

! **viel** (*much, a lot of, many*) and **wenig** (*little, not much*) usually have no endings in the singular, but normal endings in the plural:

z.B. Die Engländer trinken **viel** Tee.
The English drink a lot of tea.

BUT Vielen Dank!
Many thanks!

Sie essen **viele** Pommes frites.
They eat a lot of chips.

Ich habe **wenig** Freizeit.
I have little/not much free time.

Er hat **wenige** Freunde.
He has few friends.

2.13 ● Adjectives formed from the names of towns and cities

These adjectives end in **-er** – an ending which never varies in any way:
z.B. Die **Londoner** Busse sind rot.
The London buses are red.

die **Hamburger** U-Bahn
the Hamburg underground

One adjective from a country is made in this way: **Schweizer** (*Swiss*)

z.B. Ich habe eine **Schweizer** Uhr gekauft.
I have bought a Swiss watch.

2.14 ● Adjectives and adverbs

What is an adverb?

Just as adjectives give more information about nouns, so adverbs do the same for verbs. In German a large group of words play a double role – they are both adjectives *and* adverbs.

z.B.

| adjective | Du bist eine **gute** Fahrerin.
You are a good driver. |
| adverb | Du fährst sehr **gut**.
You drive very well. |
| adjective | Du bist ein **langsamer** Leser.
You are a slow reader. |
| adverb | Du liest **langsam**.
You read slowly. |

NOTE that when used as an adverb the word has no ending.

Remember that an adjective also has no ending when it stands alone (see 2.2):

z.B. Jan ist **intelligent**.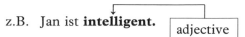

adjective

17

2.15 ● How to compare

(a) The comparative

In English we compare by adding -er to adjectives, or by using the word *more*:

> e.g. Peter is **younger** than John, but John is **more childish**.

German uses only the first method:

> z.B. Brigitte ist **intelligenter als** Ulrike.
> Brigitte is **more intelligent than** Ulrike.

NOTE that **als** is used for *than*.

Some common short adjectives (and adverbs such as **oft**) add Umlaut as well as **-er**. These are the ones you are likely to need:

alt/älter	*old/older (elder)*	kalt/kälter	*cold/colder*
jung/jünger	*young/younger*	hart/härter	*hard/harder*
lang/länger	*long/longer*	arm/ärmer	*poor/poorer*
kurz/kürzer	*short/shorter*	scharf/schärfer	*sharp/sharper*
stark/stärker	*strong/stronger*	schmal/schmäler	*narrow/narrower*
schwach/schwächer	*weak/weaker*	gesund/gesünder	*healthy/healthier*
klug/klüger	*clever/cleverer*	groß/größer	*big/bigger, tall/taller*
dumm/dümmer	*stupid/more stupid*	nah/näher	*near/nearer*
warm/wärmer	*warm/warmer*	oft/öfter	*often/more often*

Some short adjectives do *not* add Umlaut (although you might expect them to!):

> z.B. froher *happier* runder *rounder*
> fauler *lazier* schlanker *slimmer*
> flacher *flatter* voller *fuller*
> klarer *clearer*

These comparatives of adjectives and adverbs are irregular:

> gut/besser *good/better*
> viel/mehr *much/more*
> hoch/höher *high/higher*
> gern/lieber *gladly/by preference* (used to express liking – see 12.4)

Comparatives are used in the same way as other adjectives. This means that they need adjective endings when they come before a noun:

> z.B. Dieser Pullover ist **billiger** als der. (no ending needed)
> This pullover is cheaper than that one.
>
> Ich kaufe den **billigeren** Pullover. (normal adj. ending)
> I'll buy the cheaper pullover.

18

(b) Other methods of comparison – using *wie*

z.B. Margarine schmeckt nicht **so gut wie** Butter.
Margarine does not taste **as** good **as** butter.

Du schwimmst **genauso** gut **wie** ich.
You swim **just as** well **as** I do.

Peter hat **fast soviel** Geld **wie** Uwe.
Peter has **almost as much** money **as** Uwe.

2.16 ● **The superlative**

In English we add -*est* to adjectives, or we use the word *most*:

e.g. Karen gets the **biggest** salary, yet Anne is the **most
conscientious** employee.

German uses only the first method, but usually adds **-st-** not **-est-** to the
adjective:

z.B. Udo ist der **faulste** Schüler der Klasse. (NOTE: normal adj. ending)
Udo is the **laziest** pupil in the class.

The adjectives which add Umlaut in the comparative also add Umlaut in
the superlative (see list in 2.15):

z.B. Susanne ist das **jüngste** Mädchen der Klasse.
Susanne is the **youngest** girl in the class.

To make the pronunciation of superlatives easier, -est- is added to some
adjectives. Typically, these are adjectives which end in **-t, -d, -s, -ß, -z,
-sch**:

z.B. der intelligent**e**ste Junge
the most intelligent boy

der süß**e**ste Wein
the sweetest wine

Often the superlative does not precede a noun, it comes elsewhere in the
sentence. Then the usual form is **am -sten**:

Äpfel sind teuer, Birnen sind teurer, aber Melonen sind **am teuersten**.
Apples are dear, pears are dearer but melons are **the dearest**.

Jan läuft schnell, Uwe läuft schneller, aber Falk läuft **am schnellsten**.
Jan runs fast, Uwe runs faster, but Falk runs **the fastest**.

Irregular superlatives

> **gut → besser → der beste/am besten**
> good → better → the best/best

> **viel → mehr → der meiste/am meisten**
> much → more → the most/most

> **hoch → höher → der höchste/am höchsten**
> high → higher → the highest/highest

> **groß → größer → der größte/am größten**
> big → bigger → the biggest/biggest OR tall → taller → the tallest/tallest

> **nah → näher → der nächste/am nächsten**
> near → nearer → the nearest OR the next

> **gern → lieber → am liebsten**
> (used to express liking – see 12.4)

2.17 ● Special uses of *der/die/das*

(a) Often used with nouns which have an abstract or generalised sense:

> z.B. **Die** Natur ist schön.
> Nature is beautiful.

(b) With parts of the body or clothing, when the owner is obvious:

> z.B. Ich habe mir **die** Hände gewaschen.
> I washed **my** hands.

(See also 10.7.b)

(c) With days, months, seasons, meals and streets:

> z.B. **am** (= an **dem**) Mittwoch   *on Wednesday*
> **im** (= in **dem**) Januar   *in January*
> **im** (= in **dem**) Sommer   *in Summer*
> nach **dem** Frühstück   *after breakfast*
> er wohnt in **der** Goethestraße   *he lives in Goethestrasse*

(d) To express price per quantity
(See also 6.6.c.)

> z.B. Die Kartoffeln kosten neunzig Pfennig **das** Kilo.
> The potatoes cost ninety Pfennigs **a** kilo.

(e) With certain countries
With most countries, **der/die/das** is not needed (i.e. no different from English):

> z.B. Ich fahre **nach Deutschland.**
> I'm going **to Germany.**
>
> Ich komme **aus England.**
> I come **from England.**
>
> Ich wohne **in Schottland.**
> I live **in Scotland.**

However, there are a few exceptions, a common example of which is **die Schweiz** (*Switzerland*):

> z.B. Ich fahre **in die** Schweiz. (not 'nach')
> I'm going to Switzerland.
>
> Urs kommt **aus der** Schweiz.
> Urs comes from Switzerland.
>
> Er wohnt **in der** Schweiz.
> He lives in Switzerland.

Other similar ones are:

> **die** Bundesrepublik   *West Germany (the Federal Republic)*
> **die** DDR   *East Germany (the German Democratic Republic)*
> **die** Sowjetunion   *the Soviet Union*
> **die** Tschechoslowakei   *Czechoslovakia*
> **die** Niederlande (pl.)   *the Netherlands*
> **die** USA (pl.)   *the USA*

(f) In some set phrases:

> z.B. Ich gehe in **die** Schule.   *I go to school.*
> Wir sind in **der** Schule.   *We are at school.*
> Ich gehe in **die** Stadt.   *I'm going to town/into town.*
> Wir waren in **der** Stadt.   *We were in town.*
> Ich gehe **ins** Bett.   *I'm going to bed.*
> Bleiben Sie **im** Bett!   *Stay in bed!*
> Ich gehe in **die** Kirche.   *I'm going to church.*
> Ich fahre mit **dem** Bus, usw.   *I'm going by bus, etc*

2.18 ● Omission of *ein*

(a) After the verbs **sein** and **werden** to show jobs or nationalities:

> z.B. Mein Vater ist Arzt.
> My father is **a** doctor.
>
> Ich will Architektin werden.
> I want to become **an** architect.
>
> Ich bin Engländer/in.
> I'm **an** Englishman/woman.

(b) In some set phrases:

> z.B. Ich habe Fieber.
> I've got **a** temperature.
>
> Ich habe Kopfschmerzen.
> I've got **a** headache.

cases
and
prepositions

3.1 ● What are cases?

Look at these four English examples:

1 **My uncle** visits us often.
2 We often telephone **my uncle**.
3 At Christmas I gave **my uncle** a present.
4 We spent the holiday **with my uncle**.

The words *my uncle* stay exactly the same in all four sentences, even though grammatically *my uncle* has a different role in each sentence.

1 In the first sentence, *my uncle* is the *subject* – the person or thing that 'does' the action expressed by the verb (here, it is the uncle who 'does' the visiting).

2 In the second sentence, *my uncle* is the *direct object* – the person or thing on the receiving end of the action (the verb *telephone*); here it is the uncle who 'gets' telephoned.

3 In the third sentence, *my uncle* is the *indirect object*. The verb used here (*gave* from the verb *give*) can have two objects. The thing actually given (*a present*) is the direct object, and *my uncle* is the indirect object – the person or thing that the action is done *for* or *to*. Another way of saying this sentence would be: At Christmas I gave a present *to* my uncle.

4 In the fourth sentence, *my uncle* has yet another role – in a phrase introduced by a *preposition* (here it is the preposition *with*).

In English, we mostly rely on the order of words to make clear what is the subject, what is the direct object, etc. German does more than this, however:

> z.B. Der Hund biß den Briefträger.
> The dog bit the postman.

Here, *the dog* is the subject (it 'does' the biting) and *the postman* is the direct object (he 'gets' bitten). If we alter the order of words in the English version, we completely alter the meaning!

> The postman bit the dog.

But the German sentence can be rearranged without affecting the meaning:

> Den Briefträger biß der Hund.

This still means *The dog bit the postman*. German is here not relying on the order of words. It uses its *cases* to show the subject and direct object. The markers (for details see section 2) **den** and **der** show the roles played by the postman and the dog.

There are four cases: nominative, accusative, genitive, dative. Their various uses are dealt with in the following sections. (For details of the marker and adjective endings associated with the cases, see 2.4–2.9. For details of pronouns in the various cases, see 4.1–4.5.)

⊶ 3.2 • **Nominative**

(a) The nominative is the form found in dictionaries and vocabulary lists:

> z.B. der Mann, die Frau, das Kind

(b) It must be used to show the *subject* of a sentence. The subject is the person or thing that 'does' the action expressed by the verb.

> z.B. **Mein kleiner Bruder** kaufte einen neuen Kassettenrecorder.
> **My little brother** bought a new cassette recorder.

| ! |

It need not come before the verb:

> z.B. Gestern kaufte **mein kleiner Bruder** einen neuen Kassettenrecorder.
> Yesterday **my little brother** bought a new cassette recorder.

(c) The nominative is used after the verbs **sein** (*to be*) and **werden** (*to become*):

> z.B. Herr Meyer ist **ein alter Lehrer**.
> Herr Meyer is an old teacher.
>
> Mein Bruder will **Beamter** werden.
> My brother wants to become a civil servant.

| ! |

Avoid the common mistake of using accusative after these two verbs!

3.3 • **Accusative**

(a) The main use of the accusative is to show the *direct object* of a sentence. The direct object is the person or thing that is on the 'receiving end' of the verb:

z.B. Petra hat **einen Rucksack** gekauft.
Petra has bought **a rucksack**.

The rucksack is the direct object here because it is the thing that 'gets' bought.

Direct objects are not always as easy to spot as in the example given above – it is not always the item following the verb! Here are some examples of slightly less obvious direct objects:

Gestern abend hat ein Einbrecher **unseren Fernseher** gestohlen.
Yesterday evening, a burglar stole **our television set**.

Wen hast du besucht?
Whom did you visit?

Welchen Dom hast du besichtigt? (see also 2.5)
Which cathedral did you look round?

Der Pullover, **den** ich gekauft habe, ist grau. (see also 9.9)
The pullover (that) I have bought is grey.

(b) The accusative is also used after some prepositions – see 3.4 and 3.7.

(c) The accusative is used in some time expressions – see 7.6.

(d) The accusative is used in some expressions of measurement – see 6.7.

3.4 • **Prepositions with the accusative**
What are prepositions?
Prepositions are words used before nouns and pronouns to show various kinds of connections and relationships between the items in sentences. Some English examples are: *with, for, under, between, before, after, in.*

These five German prepositions 'trigger off' the accusative in the words that follow them:

durch	*through*	für	*for*	um	*around*
gegen	*against*	ohne	*without*		

z.B. Wir wanderten **durch den Wald**.
We hiked **through the wood**.

Das ist ein Geschenk **für dich**.
This is a present **for you**.

Ich spielte **gegen meinen Bruder**.
I played **against my brother**.

Geht **ohne mich** ins Kino!
Go to the cinema **without me**.

Wir saßen **um den Eßtisch**.
We sat **around the dining-table**.

NOTE that **entlang** (*along*) also takes the accusative, but it follows the word it refers to:

z.B. Gehen Sie **diese Straße entlang**.
Go **along this street**.

3.5 • Dative

(a) The main use of the dative is to show the *indirect object* of a sentence. Some verbs can have two objects – one direct object (see 3.1 and 3.3) and one indirect object. With these verbs, the indirect object is the person or thing that the action is done *for* or *to*. Here are some English examples with the verbs and indirect objects emphasised in bold type:

I **gave my sister** a calculator.

I **wrote my penfriend** a long letter.

I **showed my parents** the photos I had taken.

Here are the same examples in German. The indirect objects are in the dative (in bold type):

Ich schenkte **meiner Schwester** einen Taschenrechner.

Ich schrieb **meinem Brieffreund** einen langen Brief.

Ich zeigte **meinen Eltern** die Fotos, die ich gemacht hatte.

Dative forms always involve the endings **-em** or **-m** (m. and neut. sing.)

-er or **-r** (f. sing.)

and **-en** or **-n** (pl.)

See the tables of endings in 2.4–2.6.

In the dative plural, nouns add **-n** to their plural form, unless this already ends in **-n** or in **-s** (see 1.5).

| ! | Indirect objects are not always easy to spot. Here are some examples of less obvious indirect objects:

> **Wem** hast du das Buch gegeben?
> **To whom** have you given the book? (in conversation: Who have you given the book to?)

> Die Brieffreundin, **der** ich die Karte geschickt habe, wohnt in Wien.
> The penfriend I sent the card to (**to whom** I sent the card) lives in Vienna.

(b) The dative is also used after some prepositions – see 3.6 and 3.7.

(c) Some verbs are followed by the dative (although you would expect a direct object in the accusative!) – see 10.30.

3.6 ● Prepositions with the dative

What are prepositions? (see 3.4)

These nine prepositions always 'trigger off' the dative in the words which follow them:

aus *out of, from*
außer *apart from, except*
bei *with, at, at the house of, near*
gegenüber *opposite*
mit *with*
nach *after; to* (with place names – see 3.8)
seit *since, for* (see 7.3)
von *of, from*
zu *to* (see 3.8)

z.B. Um acht gehe ich **aus dem Haus**.
At eight I go **out of the house**.

Außer dir fahren alle mit.
Apart from you, everybody's going.

Ich wohnte **bei meinem Onkel**.
I stayed/lived **with my uncle** (**at my uncle's house**).

Wir wohnen **gegenüber der Bank**.
We live **opposite the bank**.

Ich fahre **mit meinen Eltern** hin.
I'm going there **with my parents**.

Nach dem Frühstück gehe ich zur Schule.
After breakfast I go to school.

Ich lerne Deutsch **seit drei Jahren**.
I've been learning German **for three years**.

Das ist ein Brief **von der Bank**.
This is a letter **from the bank**.

Das ist das Auto **von meiner Mutter**.
This is **my mother's** car.

Ich gehe **zum** (= **zu dem**) **Bahnhof**.
I'm going **to the station**.

Short forms

These are not compulsory, but they are usual:

$$bei + dem \longrightarrow \textbf{beim}$$
$$von + dem \longrightarrow \textbf{vom}$$
$$zu + dem \longrightarrow \textbf{zum}$$
$$zu + der \longrightarrow \textbf{zur}$$

NOTES

1 **gegenüber** often follows the word it refers to: Wir wohnen **der Bank gegenüber**.

[!] 2 **zu** means *at* not *to* in the phrase **zu Hause** (*at home*).

3 **beim** *is* compulsory before an infinitive in expressions like

    beim Essen   *while eating*
    beim Tanzen *while dancing*.

[!] **'with' – *mit* or *bei*?**

mit is the most general word for *with*:

    z.B. Ralf ging **mit Petra** ins Kino.
          Ralf went to the cinema **with Petra**.

          Ich esse Steak **mit Salat**.
          I'm having steak **with salad**.

bei must be used when the meaning is *near*, *at the same place as* or *at the house of*:

    z.B. Ich wohnte **bei meiner Tante**.
          I stayed/lived **with my aunt** (=**at my aunt's house**).

          Ich stand **bei meiner Schwester**.
          I stood **near my sister**.

          Ich stand **bei meinem Koffer**.
          I stood **near/by my suitcase**.

NOTE that **bei** cannot be used to mean '*to the house of*'. For this meaning, use **zu**:

    z.B. Ich gehe **zu meiner Tante**.
          I'm going **to my aunt's**.

NOTE also that **bei** is used in some job situations:

    z.B. Ich arbeite **bei der Post**.
          I work **for the post office**.

          Sie arbeitet **bei einer Bank**.
          She works **for a bank**.

German makes a clear distinction between *motion from place to place* and *position*. NOTE that motion within one place counts as position:

> Wir schwammen **im Fluß**.
> We swam **in the river**.

The nine prepositions which take *accusative to show motion* and *dative to show position*:

an		*at, on, up to*	über		*over, above; across*
auf		*on, on top of*	unter		*under; among*
hinter		*behind*	vor		*in front of, outside; before*
in		*in, into, to* (compare 3.8)	zwischen		*between*
neben		*next to, beside*			

Examples

Accusative – motion

Gehen Sie **an die Kasse**!
Go **to the cash-desk**.

Stell das **auf den Tisch**!
Put that **on the table**!

Der Lehrer ging **hinter den Tisch**.
The teacher **went behind the desk**.

Ich gehe **in die Küche**.
I'm going **in the kitchen**.

Dative – position

Man zahlt **an der Kasse**.
You pay **at the cash-desk**.

Das Brot ist **auf dem Tisch**.
The bread is **on the table**.

Der Lehrer stand **hinter dem Tisch**.
The teacher stood **behind the desk**.

Ich koche **in der Küche**.
I'm cooking **in the kitchen**.

über

NOTE that as well as meaning *over*, *above* and *across*, **über** is also used to mean *about*. When it means *about*, it always takes the accusative:

> z.B. Wir gingen **über die Brücke**.
> We went **over/across the bridge**.
>
> Wir gingen **über die Straße**.
> We went **across the road**/We crossed the road.
>
> Das ist ein Buch **über die Deutschen**.
> This is a book **about the Germans**.

Short forms

These are the common ones. They are not compulsory, but they are usual:

an	+ das	⟶ **ans**		in	+ das	⟶ **ins**
an	+ dem	⟶ **am**		in	+ dem	⟶ **im**
auf	+ das	⟶ **aufs**				

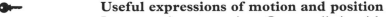

Useful expressions of motion and position
In many other expressions German distinguishes motion and position. Here are a few examples:

Motion	Position
Komm **hierher!**/Komm **her!**★	Wir wohnen **hier.**
Come **here!**	We live **here.**
Wir gingen gestern **dorthin/dahin/hin.**★	Wir waren gestern **dort/da.**
We went **there** yesterday.	We were **there** yesterday.
Ich gehe **nach Hause.**	Um fünf komme ich **zu Hause** an.
I'm going **home.**	At five o'clock I arrive (at) **home.**
Wir fahren **aufs** (= **auf das**) **Land.**	Wir wohnen **auf dem Land/Lande.**
We're going **to the country(side).**	We live **in the country(side).**
Ich fahre **ins Ausland.**	Ich möchte gern **im Ausland** wohnen.
I'm going **abroad.**	I'd like to live **abroad.**
Ich gehe **nach oben.**	Mein Zimmer ist **oben.**
I'm going **upstairs.**	My room is **upstairs.**
Ich gehe **nach unten.**	Das Wohnzimmer ist **unten.**
I'm going **downstairs.**	The living-room is **downstairs.**

★For details of **hin** and **her**, see 10.6.b.

3.8 ● How to express 'to'

! (a) **nach** is used with place names:

> z.B. Ich fahre **nach Wien.**
> I'm going **to Vienna.**
>
> Ich fahre **nach Italien.**
> I'm going **to Italy.**

EXCEPTION: countries which have **die/der** before them (see 2.17.e).

> z.B. Ich fahre **in die Schweiz.**
> I'm going **to Switzerland.**
>
> Ich fahre **in die USA.**
> I'm going **to the United States.**

(b) **zu** + *dative* is used in most other instances:

> z.B. Ich gehe **zur Post.**
> I'm going **to the post-office.**
>
> Ich gehe **zum Bahnhof.**
> I'm going **to the station.**

(c) **in** + *accusative* is used to express going to a place, then going inside the place for a while:

> z.B. Ich gehe **ins Kino.**
> I'm going **to the cinema.**
>
> Ich gehe **ins Restaurant.**
> I'm going **to the restaurant**/I'm going out for a meal.

If **zum** were used instead of **ins** in these examples, it would give the impression of going to the cinema – but without seeing a film; or of going to the restaurant – but without going in for a meal.

(d) **auf** + *accusative* is used in a few fixed phrases such as:

> z.B. Ich gehe **auf die Toilette**.
> I'm going **to the toilet**.
>
> Wir fahren **aufs Land**.
> We're going **to the country**.

3.9 ● Genitive

The genitive is the least common of the four German cases. It almost always corresponds to the meaning *of*:

> z.B. Hans ist der Sohn **eines spanischen Kellners**.
> Hans is the son **of a Spanish waiter**.
>
> Das ist ein Foto **der neuen Brücke**.
> This is a photo **of the new bridge**.

German normally uses the genitive even where English uses *'s* instead of the word *of*:

> z.B. Das ist das Auto **meines Vaters**.
> That is **my father's** car. (=the car **of my father**)

The exception is when a person is referred to by name. (There is no apostrophe.)

> z.B. Das ist Dieter**s** Auto.
> That is Dieter's car.
>
> Das ist Frau Schmidt**s** Auto.
> That is Frau Schmidt's car.
>
> Das ist Herr**n** Schmidt**s** Auto. (see 1.6)
> That is Herr Schmidt's car.

Genitive forms always involve the endings **-es** (m. and neut. sing.) or **-er** (f. sing. and pl. for all genders) on markers. Remember that masculine and neuter singular nouns add **-s** or **-es** in the genitive. Generally, short words add **-es** and longer words add **-s**, but this is not a strict rule.

> z.B. ein Foto **des** Kindes/Kinds   *a photo of the child*
> ein Foto **des** Bahnhof**s**   *a photo of the railway station*

Avoiding the genitive
In conversation, the genitive is regarded as slightly stilted and old-fashioned. It is often avoided and replaced by **von** + *dative*:

> z.B. Das ist das Auto **von meinem Vater**.
>   = Das ist das Auto **meines Vaters**.
>   That is **my father's** car.

3.10 ● Prepositions with the genitive

There are just four common prepositions with the genitive that you need to know:

statt *instead of*   trotz *in spite of*

während *during*   wegen *because of*

z.B. **Statt einer Jacke** kaufte ich einen Anorak.
Instead of a jacket I bought an anorak.

Trotz des schlechten Wetters gingen wir schwimmen.
In spite of the bad weather, we went swimming.

Während der Ferien arbeitete ich bei der Post.
During the holidays I worked for the post office.

Wegen des Nebels mußten wir sehr langsam fahren.
Because of the fog, we had to drive very slowly.

⟨!⟩ 3.11 ● Distinguishing prepositions, adverbs and conjunctions: 'before' and 'after'

English speakers who learn German often get confused by the various words for *before* (**vor, vorher, bevor**) and *after* (**nach, nachher, nachdem**).

(a) **vor** and **nach** are prepositions. They occur before nouns or pronouns:

z.B. Ich wasche mich **vor dem Frühstück**.
I have a wash **before breakfast**.

Nach dem Film gehen wir essen.
After the film, we'll go for a meal.

Nach Ihnen!
After you!

(b) **vorher** and **nachher** are adverbs of time. They mean *beforehand* and *afterwards*:

z.B. Wir gehen ins Kino, aber **vorher** gehen wir essen.
We'll go to the cinema, but **before(hand)** we'll go for a meal.

Wir gehen einkaufen, und **nachher** gehen wir schwimmen
We'll go shopping, and **afterwards** we'll go swimming.

(c) **bevor** and **nachdem** are conjunctions. They link two clauses (see 9.3 and 9.8).

z.B. **Bevor** ich meine Hausaufgaben mache, esse ich zu Abend.
Before I do my homework, I have my evening meal.

Nachdem ich mich gewaschen hatte, trocknete ich mich ab.
After I had had a wash, I dried myself.

pronouns

4

> Many pronouns are covered in other parts of the *Handbook*. For example, *question words* are covered in section 5; *relative pronouns* are covered in 9.9.

4.1 ● What is a pronoun?

Pronouns are short words which we use in place of nouns. They are a form of shorthand to help us avoid repetition. Look at these two sentences:

> **Alison** is eighteen.   **Alison** lives in London and works in a bank.

They are obviously very repetitious as they stand. We can improve them by using the pronoun *she* to replace *Alison* in the second sentence:

> Alison is eighteen.   **She** lives in London and works in a bank.

She is only one of many pronouns. In these further examples, the pronouns are emphasised in bold type:

> I'd like you to meet Martin. **He** comes from Germany.
>
> My car's gone! I think **it**'s been stolen!
>
> I'll take you swimming. Would you like **that**?
>
> Have you any street maps? Good, I'd like **one**, please.

4.2 Personal pronouns

As the name suggests, these are pronouns which refer to *people*. (In fact, they can also refer to *things*, see 4.4). German pronouns can occur in various cases, in a similar way to nouns. For details of the cases and their uses, see section 3. The following examples show the German pronoun for *he* in its various cases:

> Hast du Jochen gesehen?
> Have you seen Jochen?
>
> Wo ist **er**?
> Where is **he**?
>
> Hast du **ihn** gesehen?
> Have you seen **him**?
>
> Ich soll mit **ihm** Tennis spielen.
> I'm supposed to be playing tennis with **him**.

er is nominative, **ihn** is accusative and **ihm** is dative.

(a) The following table shows all the personal pronouns in nominative, accusative and dative. Genitive pronouns are not shown here because they are very rarely used.

! The right-hand box shows the markers **mein, dein**, etc. (equivalents of *my, your*, etc.) to help you distinguish them from the pronouns. Take care on this point (see also 2.7).

	nom.	acc.	dat.	marker	
I, me	ich	mich	mir	mein	*my*
you	du	dich	dir	dein	*your*
he, him; it	er	ihn	ihm	sein	*his, its*
she, her; it	sie	sie	ihr	ihr	*her, its*
it	es	es	ihm	sein	*its*
we, us	wir	uns	uns	unser	*our*
you	ihr	euch	euch	euer	*your*
you	Sie	Sie	Ihnen	Ihr	*your*
they, them	sie	sie	ihnen	ihr	*their*

You will notice that there are three sets of pronouns corresponding to *you*, and these are explained in the next section (4.3). The pronouns for *he, she* and *it* are explained in 4.4.

(b) *man*

The pronoun **man** means *one* (as in *What does one do in this situation?*), and can refer to either sex. Whereas it is often associated with upper-class speech in English, it is freely used by everyone who speaks German. In English we often say instead *you* or *they*:

z.B. Was **macht man** in dieser Situation?
What **does one do**/What **do you do** in this situation?

Man sagt, daß Portugal sehr schön ist.
They say that Portugal is very beautiful.

The verb forms used are the same as those used with **er/sie/es**. The accusative is **einen**, the dative is **einem** and the possessive (*one's*) is **sein**. However, these forms occur relatively rarely.

! Do not confuse **man** with **der Mann**.

33

All three of these pronouns mean *you.*

(a) *du*

Use **du** (and **dich, dir, dein** – see the table in 4.2) when speaking to any one person whom you address by first name. Children and teenagers automatically use **du** to each other, whether they are already friends or not. **du** is also always used when speaking to relatives. In letter-writing, **Du, Dich, Dir** and **Dein** must be written with a capital letter.

z.B.   Wie alt bist **du**, Beate?
How old are you, Beate?

Kann ich **dich** morgen besuchen?
Can I visit you tomorrow?

Wie geht es **dir**? (see 10.30.d)
How are you?

Wie ist **deine** Adresse?
What's your address?

(b) *ihr*

Use **ihr** (and **euch, euer** – see the table in 4.2) when speaking to any two or more people to whom you would say **du**. **ihr** is simply the plural of **du**. **ihr** is also used when speaking to a mixture of people to whom you say **du** and **Sie**. In letter-writing, **Ihr, Euch** and **Euer** must be written with a capital letter.

z.B.   Wie alt seid **ihr**, Beate und Rolf?
How old are you, Beate and Rolf?

Kann ich **euch** morgen besuchen?
Can I visit you tomorrow?

Wie geht es **euch**?
How are you (= you two/you all)?

Wie ist **euere** Adresse?
What's your address?

(c) *Sie*

Use **Sie** (and **Ihnen, Ihr** – see the table in 4.2) when speaking to any person or people with whom you are not on first-name terms. This means that you use **Sie** when speaking to adult strangers and other adults in positions of authority (such as teachers or policemen). These are all people whom you address as **Herr** (*Mr*), **Frau** (*Mrs* or *Ms*) or **Fräulein** (*Miss*). **Sie, Ihnen** and **Ihr** must *always* be written with a capital letter.

z.B.   Wie alt sind **Sie**, Herr Schmidt?
How old are you, Herr Schmidt?

Kann ich **Sie** morgen besuchen?
Can I visit you tomorrow?

Wie geht es **Ihnen**?
How are you?

Wie ist **Ihre** Adresse?
What's your address?

4.4 • How to use *er, sie* and *es*

These three pronouns (and their accusative, dative and marker forms – see 4.2) do not correspond exactly to the English pronouns *he, she* and *it*. This is because things as well as people have genders in German (see 1.2).

> **er** refers to any masculine noun
> **sie** refers to any feminine noun
> **es** refers to neuter nouns (BUT **sie** is used when referring to **das Fräulein**)

> z.B. Das ist **mein neuer Volkswagen. Er** ist schön, nicht wahr? Ich habe **ihn** gestern gekauft.
> This is **my new Volkswagen. It**'s lovely, isn't it? I bought **it** yesterday.

> Das ist **meine neue Jacke. Sie** ist schön, nicht wahr? Ich habe **sie** gestern gekauft.
> This is **my new jacket. It**'s lovely, isn't it? I bought **it** yesterday.

> Das ist **mein neues Fahrrad. Es** ist schön, nicht wahr? Ich habe **es** gestern gekauft.
> This is **my new bicycle. It**'s lovely, isn't it? I bought **it** yesterday.

> [!] Beware of the common mistake of using **es** when referring to masculine or feminine nouns.

4.5 • Ways of expressing 'this' and 'that'

(a) **das** is the most general word, and it is used for both *this* and *that*:

> z.B. Was ist **das**?
> What's this/that?

> **Das** macht Spaß!
> This/that is fun.

> **Das** ist nett von dir.
> That's nice of you.

When referring back to a specific noun which has been mentioned previously, use **dieser/diese/dieses** for *this*, and **der/die/das** for *that*.

(b) **dieser/diese/dieses**. For details of the endings used here, see 2.5.

> z.B. Ich möchte einen neuen Pullover. **Dieser** ist schön, aber **diese** sind schöner.
> I'd like a new pullover. **This (one)** is nice, but **these (ones)** are nicer.

(c) **der/die/das** can be used as pronouns to mean *that*, as well as the usual meaning of *the*. The endings are as shown in 2.4 except for the dative plural which is **denen** instead of **den**.

> z.B. Ich möchte einen neuen Pullover. **Der** ist schön, aber **die** sind schöner.
> I'd like a new pullover. **That (one)** is nice, but **those (ones)** are nicer.

35

4.6 ● *das* or *daß*?

!   **das** and **daß** both correspond to *that* in English.
One use of **das** is described above in 4.5:

         Das ist ein Foto von meiner Mutter.
         That's a photo of my mother.

das can also be a relative pronoun meaning *that* or *which* (see 9.9):

         Das Haus, **das** ich gekauft habe, . . .
         The house **that** (= which) I have bought . . .

daß is a conjunction which opens subordinate clauses (see 9.8):

         Peter sagt, **daß** er mitkommen will.
         Peter says **that** he wants to come along.

         Jan ist so dumm, **daß** er . . .
         Jan is so stupid **that** he . . .

4.7 ● *einer/eine/eines* as pronouns

You already know the marker **ein/eine/ein** (see 2.6). There is also a pronoun with slightly different endings, **einer/eine/eines**:

	m.	f.	neut.	
nom.	**einer**	eine	**eines**	In conversation often shortened to **eins**.
acc.	einen	eine	**eines**	
gen.	eines	einer	eines	
dat.	einem	einer	einem	

You will notice that most of the table is the same as that for the marker **ein/eine/ein**. The forms which are different are emphasised in bold type in the table. Here is an example of this pronoun in use:

     Da sind die zwei Jungen. **Einer** heißt Holger, und der andere heißt Roland.
     There are the two boys. **One** is called Holger and the other is called Roland.

'one of the . . .'

einer/eine/eines is also often used in this way:

         Einer der Jungen stürzte und brach sich das Bein.
         One of the boys fell and broke his leg.

einer is nominative, the subject of the verb **stürzte**. **der Jungen** is genitive plural: *of the boys*.

4.8 ● **How to say 'mine', 'yours', 'his', 'hers', etc.**

These pronouns are based on the markers **mein**, **dein**, **sein**, etc. (see 2.7 and 4.2), but with the same endings as those used on the pronoun **einer/eine/eines** in 4.7.

      z.B. ● Wo sind unsere Koffer?
             ○ Da ist **meiner**, und hier ist **deiner**.

4.9 ● *da-* **with prepositions:** *davon, darin,* **etc.**

When in English *it* or *them* follow prepositions, and refer to things and not people, in German **da-** is used instead of the usual pronoun. These examples should make the point clear:

      Das ist ein Foto von meinem Bruder. ⟶ Das ist ein Foto **von ihm**.
      This is a photo of my brother.   ⟶ This is a photo **of him**.

      Das ist ein Foto von meinem VW-Polo. ⟶ Das ist ein Foto **davon**.
      This is a photo of my VW Polo.   ⟶ This is a photo **of it**.

This does not depend on gender (both the brother and the VW Polo are masculine in German), but on the fact that the brother is a person and the car is a thing. The system with **da-** can be used for plural things, too:

      Das ist ein Foto von meinen Pflanzen. ⟶ Das ist ein Foto **davon**.
      This is a photo of my plants.   ⟶ This is a photo **of them**.

da- can be added to most prepositions.
When the preposition starts with a vowel, we add **dar-**:

      z.B. Mein Name war in meinem Mantel. ⟶ Mein Name war **darin**.
            My name was in my overcoat.   ⟶ My name was **in it**.

4.10 ● **Omission of pronouns: verbs with the prefix** *mit-*

With verbs such as **mit**kommen, **mit**gehen, **mit**fahren and **mit**nehmen, German does not need the pronoun that we always put in in English:

      z.B. Kommst du mit?
            Are you coming **with me/us**?

            Ich will mitgehen.
            I want to go **with you/him/them**, etc.

            Ich bin mitgefahren.
            I went **with you/her/them**, etc.

            Können Sie mich mitnehmen?
            Can you take me **with you**? (i.e. Can you give me a lift?)

4.11 ● **How to say 'nothing new', 'something interesting', etc.**

      z.B. Ich habe **nichts Neues** gekauft.
            I bought **nothing new**.

Hat er **etwas Interessantes** gesagt?
Did he say **anything interesting**?

Haben Sie **etwas Billigeres**?
Have you **anything cheaper**?

NOTE that the adjective is given a *capital letter* and the ending **-es**.

These three common expressions with **alles** follow a slightly different pattern:

Ich wünsche dir **alles Gute**!
I wish you all the best!

Wir haben **alles mögliche** gekauft.
We bought all kinds of things. (literally: everything possible)

Du deckst den Tisch. **Alles andere** mache ich.
You lay the table. I'll do everything else.

After **alles**, the adjective ends in **-e**. **Alles mögliche** and **alles andere** have the further peculiarity that the adjective is *not* given a capital letter.

4.12 ● Other common pronouns

(a) 'some' and 'any'

Singular: **etwas**
Plural: **einige** also: **welche**

z.B. Wir haben Salat da. Möchtest du **etwas**?
We have some salad here. Would you like **some**?

Wir haben Kartoffelchips da. Möchtest du **einige/welche**?
We have some crisps here. Would you like **some**?

(b) *beide* and *die beiden*
These mean *both* or *the two of them*.

z.B. Anna und Jörg gingen **beide** ins Kino.
Anna and Jörg **both** went to the cinema.

Die beiden wollten den neuen James-Bond-Film sehen.
The two of them wanted to see the new James Bond film.

! (c) *alles* and *alle*
alles is *singular* and means *everything*. The verb must be *singular*.
alle is *plural* and means *everybody*. The verb must be *plural*.

z.B. Wir wollten in Zürich einkaufen, aber **alles war** viel zu teuer.
We wanted to do some shopping in Zürich, but **everything was** much too expensive.

Morgen fahre ich mit meiner Klasse nach Köln. **Alle sind** sehr aufgeregt.
Tomorrow I'm going to Cologne with my class. **Everybody is** very excited.

questions

Study these examples of typical German questions:

Hast du Geschwister?
Have you any brothers or sisters?

Arbeitest du in deiner Freizeit?
Do you work in your free time?

Arbeitet dein Bruder?
Does your brother work?

These are all questions which can be answered simply by **Ja** or **Nein**. They are made by turning the verb and its subject round, so that the verb starts the sentence (**Hast? Arbeitest? Arbeitet?**). English often brings in the verb *do* for this type of question (look at the English translations of the second and third of these examples: *Do you work?*, *Does your brother work?*). German does *not* do this.

Here are some more examples of typical German questions:

Wie heißt du?
What's your name?

Wo wohnst du?
Where do you live?

Was liest du?
What are you reading?

Wann kommt der Bus?
When does the bus come?

These questions are made in a similar way. NOTE that German never uses any equivalent of the verb *do* to help form the question. They start with special question words (**Wie? Wo? Was? Wann?**).

Here is a list of the question words you need to know:

was?	*what?*	woher?	*where . . . from?*
wo?	*where?*	wann?	*when?*
wer?	*who?* (nom.)	wie?	*how?* (sometimes = *what?*)
wen?	*who? whom* (acc.)	wieviel?	*how much?*
wem?	*whom? to whom?* (dat.)	wie viele?	*how many?*
wessen?	*whose?*	wie lange?	*how long?*
warum?	*why?*	was für?	*what kind of?*
wieso?	*why? ('how come?')*	womit?	*with what?*
wozu?	*what . . . for? (for what purpose?)*	wovon?	*of/from what?*
wohin?	*where (to)?*	worauf?	*on what?*

! Watch out! **wo?** = *where?* and **wer?** = *who?*

(a) **womit, wovon, worauf**, etc. are formed by adding **wo-** to prepositions
(**wor-** is added if the preposition starts with a vowel).

> z.B. **Womit** hast du das Brot geschnitten?
> **What** did you cut the bread **with**?
> (**With what** did you cut the bread?)

(b) **wessen** (*whose*).

> z.B. **Wessen Schal** ist das?
> **Whose scarf** is that?

In conversation, **wessen** is usually avoided. This example becomes:

> Wem gehört der Schal?
> To whom does that scarf belong? (Who does that scarf belong to?)

(c) **Was für** (*what kind of?*)
Was für is not followed by the accusative you would expect after **für**,
unless the phrase is the direct object of the question.

> z.B. Was für **ein** Schrank ist das?
> What kind of a cupboard is that?
>
> Was für **einen** Schrank hast du?
> What kind of a cupboard have you got?

40

numbers and amounts

6.1 • Numbers

0 null
1 eins
2 zwei (on telephone, radio, etc., often **zwo**)
3 drei
4 vier
5 fünf
6 sechs
7 sieben
8 acht
9 neun
10 zehn
11 elf
12 zwölf
13 dreizehn
14 vierzehn
15 fünfzehn
16 sechzehn
  (**sechs** drops its **s**)
17 siebzehn
  (**sieben** drops its **en**)
18 achtzehn
19 neunzehn
20 zwanzig

21 einundzwanzig
  (**eins** drops its **s**)
22 zweiundzwanzig
26 sechsundzwanzig
27 sieb**en**undzwanzig
30 dreißig
  (**dreißig** has **ß** and not **z**)
40 vierzig
50 fünfzig
60 sechzig
  (**sechs** drops its **s**)
70 siebzig
  (**sieben** drops its **en**)
80 achtzig
90 neunzig
100 hundert
  (more usual than **ein**hundert)
101 hunderteins
125 hundertfünfundzwanzig
200 zweihundert
600 sechshundert
700 sieb**en**hundert
1000 tausend
  (more usual than **ein**tausend)

3456 dreitausendvierhundertsechsundfünfzig
1984 neunzehnhundertvierundachtzig (the year)
1 000 000 eine Million

Points to remember

(a) This form – **eins** – is used when counting, and in mathematics:

z.B. Seite **eins** *page one*
zwei und **eins** ist drei *2 + 1 = 3*

When the German equivalent of *one* comes before a noun, the normal marker endings are used (see 2.6).

z.B. Ich habe nur **einen** Bruder.
I have only **one** brother.

(b) Arithmetic

zwei und drei ist fünf	sechs weniger vier ist zwei
2 + 3 = 5	6 − 4 = 2
elf mal eins ist elf	zehn durch fünf ist zwei
11 × 1 = 11	10 : 5 = 2

The last sum here shows the German division sign. It is **:** and not ÷.

(c) Telephone numbers

> z.B. Mein Telefonnummer ist fünf, sechsundzwanzig, fünfundsechzig.
> My telephone number is 5 26 65.

(d) Years

> z.B. Ich bin 1974 geboren. (Spoken as: Ich bin neunzehnhundertvierundsiebzig geboren.)

In English we say 'I was born *in* 1974', etc. Be careful not to carry '*in*' over into your German.

6.2 ● Fractions and decimals

(a) Fractions

$\frac{1}{2}$ (ein) halb	$\frac{3}{4}$ drei Viertel
$\frac{1}{3}$ ein Drittel	$1\frac{1}{2}$ eineinhalb (or the special word: anderthalb)
$\frac{1}{4}$ ein Viertel	$2\frac{1}{2}$ zweieinhalb

'half'

These examples show the most common forms:

> **ein halbes Pfund**, bitte! *half a pound, please!*
> **eine halbe Stunde** später *half an hour later*

You may also meet the noun **die Hälfte**:

> z.B. Ich aß **die Hälfte des Apfels**.
> I ate **half (of) the apple**.

(b) Decimals

German uses a comma where English uses a decimal point:

> z.B. 1,5 einskommafünf *1.5 one point five*

6.3 ● How to say 'once', 'twice', 'three times', etc.

These words are very easy to make, as these examples show:

> Kaviar habe ich nur **einmal** gegessen.
> I've only eaten caviar **once**.

> Frank hat mich **zweimal** besucht.
> Frank has visited me **twice**.

> Ich war schon **dreimal** in Deutschland.
> I've been to Germany **three times**.

6.4 ● How to say 'first', 'second', 'third', etc.

These numbers are really adjectives (e.g. the *first* girl, the *second* house), and they therefore need normal adjective endings in German.

> z.B. Der **erste** Monat ist Januar.
> The **first** month is January.
>
> Marianne war das **zweite** Mädchen.
> Marianne was the **second** girl.
>
> Der Golf ist mein **drittes** Auto.
> The Golf is my **third** car.

The others, up to tenth, are: der **vierte**
der **fünfte**
der **sechste**
der **siebte** (or: der **siebente**)
der **achte** (note: only one **t**)
der **neunte**
der **zehnte**

This system of adding **-te** to the number continues up to and including *nineteenth* (der **neunzehnte**). For all numbers after *nineteenth*, **-ste** must be added:

> z.B. der **zwanzigste**, der **einundzwanzigste**, der **hundertste**

When writing in figures, do it like this:

> z.B. der **1.** Preis **1st** prize

The full stop is compulsory. These numbers occur most often in dates (see 6.5).

6.5 ● Dates

Here are some examples:

> Der wievielte ist heute?
> What's the date today?
>
> Heute ist **der fünfte März**.
> Today is **the fifth of March**.
>
> Heute ist **der 5. März**.
> Today is **the 5th March**.

The key example is the second one. **Der fünfte** is used, as a short way of saying **der fünfte Tag** (*the fifth day*). That is why a masculine marker is used. The **-e** ending on **fünfte** is a normal adjective ending (see 2.4).

Dating letters
For the date at the top of a letter, the accusative is used:

> z.B.   Hannover, **den 4. Juni**

This is read as: 'Hannover, den **vierten** Juni.' (See also 7.6.)

Birthdays

This table shows how to say when your (or someone else's) birthday is:

NOTE that the German and English versions do *not* correspond word for word!

z.B.   Ich habe am einunddreißigsten Juli Geburtstag.
My birthday is (on) the 31st July.

'from . . . to . . .'

z.B.   Ich bleibe **vom** fünft**en bis zum** zwölft**en** September.
I'm staying **from the** fifth **to the** twelfth of September.

6.6 • Quantities and money

(a) Quantities

z.B.   Ich kaufe zwei **Kilo** Zucker.
I'm buying two kilos of sugar.

Er trank drei **Liter** Bier.
He drank three litres of beer.

Ich trank drei **Glas** Cola.
I drank three glasses of cola.

In this kind of expression, the words which show a quantity (e.g. **Kilo**, **Liter**, **Glas**, **Pfund**, etc.) do not change to show the plural. They are left in their singular form. (EXCEPTIONS: zwei Tasse**n** Tee, zwei Flasche**n** Wein.) English includes the word *of* (e.g. two kilos *of* sugar). The German expressions do *not* include any word for *of*.

44

(b) Money

z.B.

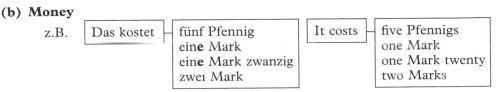

Das kostet	fünf Pfennig		It costs	five Pfennigs
	eine Mark			one Mark
	eine Mark zwanzig			one Mark twenty
	zwei Mark			two Marks

NOTE that neither **Mark** nor **Pfennig** change in the plural.

The word *Deutschmark* does not exist in German. It is an English invention! The official name for the currency is **die Deutsche Mark**, and Germans sometimes use the shortened form **D-Mark**.

The ten-Pfennig piece is often called a **Groschen (der Groschen (-))**.

East Germany, Austria and Switzerland

East Germany has its own **Mark** and **Pfennig**.
Austria uses the **Schilling (der Schilling** – ein Schilling, zwei Schilling).
Switzerland has **Franken**, divided into 100 **Rappen**
(der Franken (-), der Rappen (-)).

(c) Quantities and money

z.B. Die Kartoffeln kosten eine Mark **das** Kilo.
The potatoes cost one Mark **a** kilo.

Die Butter kostet sechs Mark **das** Pfund.
The butter costs six Marks **a** pound.

Die Bleistifte kosten fünfzig Pfennig **das** Stück.
The pencils cost fifty Pfennigs **each/a piece**.

In this kind of sentence, German uses words for *the*, where in English we usually use *a* or *per*.

6.7 ● **Measurements**

z.B. ich wiege fünfundsechzig Kilo   *I weigh 65 Kilos*
ich bin ein Meter siebzig groß   *my height is 1.70 metres*
mein Zimmer ist vier Meter lang   *my room is four metres long*
    und drei Meter breit   *and three metres wide*
mein Zimmer ist vier mal drei   *my room is four by three (metres)*

The use of the accusative in measurements
The accusative is needed in expressions like these:

Das Auto ist erst **einen Monat** alt.
The car is only one month old.

Diese Straße ist **einen Kilometer** lang.
This road is one kilometre long.

(For details of the accusative, see 3.3.)

time

7

7.1 ● Introduction

There is an enormous variety of time expressions, and they cannot all be listed here. Dates are dealt with in 6.5. For *before* and *after*, see 3.11.

7.2 ● Clock time – *Wie spät ist es?/Wieviel Uhr ist es?*

(a) The everyday method

Es ist zwei Uhr.   Es ist fünf nach zwei.   Es ist zehn nach zwei.   Es ist Viertel nach zwei.

Es ist zwanzig nach zwei.   Es ist fünf vor halb drei.   Es ist halb drei.   Es ist fünf nach halb drei.

Es ist zwanzig vor drei.   Es ist Viertel vor drei.   Es ist zehn vor drei.   Es ist fünf vor drei.

one o'clock = **ein** Uhr   five past one, etc. = fünf nach **eins**, usw.

Twenty-five past, half past and *twenty-five to* are the times which, in German, are most different from the English method of telling the time. English looks back to the previous hour (half past *two*), whereas German looks ahead to the next hour (halb **drei**). Twenty-five past is regarded as five minutes before this (*twenty-five past two* – **fünf vor halb drei**), and twenty-five to is regarded as five minutes after the half (*twenty-five to three* – **fünf nach halb drei**).

'at' + clock time

To say *at* a certain time, German uses **um**:

    z.B. Ich stehe **um** sieben Uhr auf.
        I get up **at** seven o'clock.

'at about' + clock time

To give an approximate time in German, use **gegen**:

    z.B. Ich stehe **gegen** sieben Uhr auf.
        I get up **(at) about** seven o'clock.

'Second', 'minute' and 'hour'

die Sekunde (-n) *second*
die Minute (-n) *minute*
die Stunde (-n) *hour*

> [!] Do not confuse **Stunde** and **Uhr**. **Stunde** means *hour*, **Uhr** means *clock* and *o'clock*.

(b) The 24-hour clock

This is much easier than the everyday method. It is used a lot more in German-speaking countries than in English-speaking ones. It is quite often used even in conversation. Here are some examples which show how to express times on the 24-hour clock:

Es ist zwei Uhr.	*It is 02.00 hours (2 am).*
Es ist vierzehn Uhr.	*It is 14.00 hours (2 pm).*
Es ist sechzehn Uhr fünf.	*It is 16.05 (4.05 pm).*
Es ist achtzehn Uhr fünfundzwanzig.	*It is 18.25 (6.25 pm).*

In figures, write it like this: Es ist 2 Uhr.

Es ist 14 Uhr.
Es ist 16.05 Uhr.
Es ist 18.25 Uhr.
usw.

The 24-hour clock is especially used when talking about travel arrangements:

z.B. Der Zug fährt **um zwanzig Uhr** ab.
The train leaves **at 8 pm**.

7.3 ● 'for' + time

> [!] In English we often use phrases involving *for* with an expression of time:
>
> e.g. Last night I watched TV **for two hours**.
> Tomorrow I'm going to Germany **for ten days**.
> I have been learning German **for three years**.

These three examples correspond to the three different German ways of dealing with this type of expression.

(a) In most instances, there is no equivalent of the English *for*:

z.B. Gestern abend sah ich **zwei Stunden** fern.
Last night I watched TV **for two hours**.

It is optional to add the word **lang**:

z.B. Gestern abend sah ich **zwei Stunden lang** fern.

(b) When talking about *future plans*, **für** + *accusative* is used:

z.B. Morgen fahre ich **für zehn Tage** nach Deutschland.
Tomorrow I'm going to Germany **for ten days**.

(c) To show that an activity started in the past and *continues* up to the time you are talking about, German uses **seit** + *dative*. The tenses used are different from those used in English, which generally include the words *have been* or *had been*. This pair of sentences should make the point clear:

> z.B.   Ich **lerne** Deutsch **seit drei Jahren**.
> I **have been learning** German **for three years**.

The German sentence literally says 'I am learning German since three years' – the reason for the present tense being that I am still learning German *now*, in the present.

The whole thing can be transferred into the past:

Ich **lernte** Deutsch **seit drei Jahren**, als ich nach Berlin fuhr.
I **had been learning** German **for three years**, when I went to Berlin.

The two pairs of examples above show the two German tenses that can be used in this type of sentence – *present* and *simple past*.

EXCEPTION: *negative* sentences require the *perfect* or *pluperfect*:

> z.B.   Ich **habe** ihn **seit drei Jahren nicht** mehr **gesehen**.
> I have not seen him for three years.

The point here is that the activity does *not* continue up to the present.

7.4 ● How to say 'when': *wann, als* and *wenn*

!

These often cause confusion!

(a) **wann** is a question word (see section 5), and must be used whenever a question is involved. This includes reported questions (see 10.38.c).

> z.B.   **Wann** kommst du nach Deutschland?
> **When** are you coming to Germany?
>
> Ich fragte den Schaffner, **wann** der Zug in Bonn ankommen würde.
> I asked the ticket inspector **when** the train would arrive in Bonn.
>
> Ich weiß nicht, **wann** der Film beginnt.
> I don't know **when** the film begins.

(b) For talking about *a single event in the past*, you must use **als**:

> z.B.   **Als** ich in der Schule ankam, war es schon Viertel nach neun.
> **When** I arrived at school, it was already quarter past nine.

(c) Other uses of *when* in English are covered by the German word **wenn**:

> z.B.   **Wenn** Renate ankommt, gehen wir alle ins Theater.
> **When** Renate arrives, we'll all go to the theatre.

When talking about the past, **wenn** means *whenever*:

> z.B.   **Wenn** ich in der Schule ankam, spielte ich immer Fußball mit Udo.
> **When(ever)** I arrived at school, I always used to play football with Udo.

als and **wenn** are conjunctions which introduce subordinate clauses. For more details, see 9.8.

7.5 ● **How to pinpoint times: 'in'/'on'/'at' + time**

The following sections explain various possibilities:

⚠ **(a) Years**

German simply gives the year. It is wrong to use **in . . .**

> z.B. Mein Bruder ist *1970* geboren.
> My brother was born *in 1970*.

⚠ **(b) Months and seasons**

Use **im**:

> z.B. Ich habe **im Januar** Geburtstag.
> My birthday is in January.
>
> **Im Winter** gehe ich skilaufen.
> In winter I go skiing.

The seasons: der Frühling *spring*   der Sommer *summer*
              der Herbst *autumn*   der Winter *winter*

(For the months, see 6.5.)

⚠ **(c) Days and parts of days**

Use **am** + the day (or part of the day) for one occasion. For several occasions just add **-s** to the day (or part of the day).

> z.B. **Am Samstag** gingen wir aus.
> **On Saturday**, we went out.
>
> Wir gingen **samstags** aus.
> We went out **on Saturdays**.

NOTE that in the second example, **samstags** has a small letter.

Similarly: am Montag/montags   *on Monday/Mondays*
            am Dienstag/dienstags   *on Tuesday/Tuesdays*

The days of the week, starting with *Sunday*, are:
Sonntag, Montag, Dienstag, Mittwoch, Donnerstag, Freitag, Samstag
(or, in North Germany: **Sonnabend**). All these days are masculine.

Parts of the day are treated in the same way:

am Morgen/morgens	*in the morning/mornings*
am Vormittag/vormittags	*in the morning/mornings*
am Nachmittag/nachmittags	*in the afternoon/afternoons*
am Abend/abends	*in the evening/evenings*

All these parts of the day are masculine. **Die Nacht** is treated slightly differently:

in der Nacht/nachts	*in the night/at night*

The days and parts of days can be combined, like this:

am Montagabend/montagabends	*on Monday evening/* *evenings*

Also: morgens um 10 Uhr	*at 10 o'clock in the* *morning*
um 8 Uhr abends	*at 8 o'clock in the evening*

(d) This morning, etc.

z.B. heute *today*

heute morgen *this morning*

heute abend *this evening*

morgen *tomorrow*

morgen abend *tomorrow evening*

übermorgen *the day after tomorrow*

gestern *yesterday*

gestern morgen *yesterday morning*

gestern abend *yesterday evening*

vorgestern *the day before yesterday*

For *tomorrow morning*, say **morgen früh** (*not* „morgen morgen"!)

NOTE also: am nächsten Tag *(on) the next day*

am folgenden Tag *(on) the following day*

am nächsten Morgen *(on) the next morning*

usw. *etc.*

(e) How to say 'one day', 'one morning', etc.
The following fixed expressions use the genitive:

eines Tages *one day*

eines Sonntags, usw. *one Sunday, etc.*

eines Morgens *one morning*

eines Abends *one evening*

eines Nachts *one night*

(**eines Nachts** is very odd – this genitive form looks masculine or neuter. In fact, **die Nacht** is feminine!)

To say 'one *fine* day' or 'one *foggy November* morning', change from genitive to **an** + *dative*:

z.B. an einem schönen Tag *one fine day*

an einem nebligen Novembermorgen *one foggy November morning*

7.6 ● The use of the accusative in time expressions

When there is no preposition involved and there is no reason to use any other case (as in 7.5.e), time expressions are put into the accusative. Of course, the accusative only shows up clearly with masculine nouns. The following example sentences show many of the commonest expressions:

Ich war **einen Tag** in Bonn.
I was in Bonn **for a day**.

Ich las **den ganzen Tag (lang)**.
I read **all day (long)**.

Sie arbeitet **die ganze Zeit**.
She works **all the/the whole time**.

Ich sehe **jeden Tag** fern.
I watch TV **every day**.

Sie geht **jeden Abend** aus.
She goes out **every night/evening**.

Wir fahren **jedes Jahr** nach Spanien.
We go to Spain **every year**.

Ich besuche ihn **jeden Monat**.
I visit him **every month**.

Sie kommt **nächsten Freitag**.
She's coming **next Friday**.

Sie kommt **nächste Woche**.
She's coming **next week**.

Sie kommt **nächstes Jahr**.
She's coming **next year**.

Ich war **letzten Montag** in London.
I was in London **last Monday**.

NOTE that we often say *night* in English, when we really mean *evening*. This must be **Abend** in German.

In German the accusative is used for the date in headings, for example in a letter:

Hamburg, **den 9.** (= **neunten**) **Mai**

(For more on the accusative, see 3.4 and following sections.)

7.7 ● Using *erst, zuerst, zunächst* and *erst mal*

> **!**

erst is used in time expressions, where in English we would say *only* or *not until*:

z.B. Wir kamen **erst** gestern an.
We arrived **only** yesterday./We did **not** arrive **until** yesterday.

Erst als das Telefon klingelte, wachte ich auf.
Only when (not until) the telephone rang did I wake up.

Er ist **erst** zehn Jahre alt.
He is only ten years old.

In the last example, the idea is not *not until* but *only ten years old so far*. In all these examples, **nur**, the usual word for *only* would be wrong.

zuerst is usually used for *first* meaning *at first* or *first of all*; **zunächst** can also be used but it is less common. In conversation, **erst mal** is often used for the first activity in a sequence.

z.B. **Zuerst** gingen wir einkaufen.
First (of all) we went shopping.

Essen wir **zunächst** einmal, dann . . .
Let's eat first (of all), then . . .

Ich will mich **erst mal** waschen, dann . . .
First (of all) I want to have a wash, then . . .

7.8 ● How to express 'ago'

Phrases which involve *ago* in English are expressed in German using **vor** + *dative*. (For other uses of **vor** + *dative*, see 3.7.)

z.B. Der Zug fuhr **vor einer Stunde** ab.
The train left **an hour ago**.

Wir kamen **vor zwei Tagen** an.
We arrived **two days ago**.

7.9 ● Other useful time expressions

(a) These expressions are often used to begin sentences. When they are used in this way, the main verb must follow them immediately (see 9.4).

dann	*then*	kurz danach	*shortly afterwards*
schließlich	*finally*	nach einer Weile	*after a while*
endlich	*at last*	einige Minuten später	*a few minutes later*
plötzlich	*suddenly*		
gerade in diesem Moment	*just at that moment*	währenddessen	*meanwhile*
		inzwischen	*meanwhile*
zur Zeit	*at the moment*	ohne weiteres	*without further ado*

(b) Yet more time expressions!

bis jetzt	*up to now*	immer	*always*
das nächste Mal	*next time*	nie/niemals	*never*
das letzte Mal	*last time*	stundenlang	*for hours (on end)*
zum erstenmal	*for the first time*	tagelang	*for days (on end)*
zum letztenmal	*for the last time*	rechtzeitig	*in time/on time*
diesmal	*this time*	oft	*often*
manchmal	*sometimes*	selten	*seldom, rarely*
bald	*soon*	Anfang Mai (usw.)	*at the beginning of May (etc.)*
gleich	*very soon, straightaway*	Mitte Juni (usw.)	*in the middle of June (etc.)*
sofort	*immediately*	Ende Juli (usw.)	*at the end of July (etc.)*
noch	*still*		
immer noch	*still (emphatic)*	zu Weihnachten	*at Christmas*
immer wieder	*over and over again*	zu Ostern	*at Easter*

52

particles

8.1 ● What is a particle?

A particle is something small.

In German, particles are the small words such as **schon**, **da**, **doch**, etc. with which German-speakers love to 'sprinkle' their language. A particle can affect the meaning of a sentence in quite a subtle way.

8.2 ● *ja*

As well as being the word for *yes*, **ja** (often coming in the middle of a sentence) has a range of meanings such as *really*, *after all*, *of course*. It adds emphasis to what the speaker is saying and generally conveys the idea that the speaker expects the listener to agree with, or already know, what he is saying.

> z.B. Ulli kann nicht skilaufen gehen. Er ist ja krank.
> Ulli cannot go skiing. He is ill (of course/after all).
>
> Das ist ja interessant!
> That's interesting! (isn't it?)
>
> Du weißt ja, daß ich nicht schwimmen kann.
> You know (of course) that I cannot swim.

8.3 ● *aber*

As a conjunction **aber** means *but*, and placed after the subject it often means *however*:

> z.B. Jochen war sehr nervös; Jutta **aber** blieb ganz ruhig.
> Jochen was very nervous; Jutta, **however**, remained quite calm.

The position of **aber** in this example shows an apparent exception to the 'verb second' rule (for which, see 9.4).

As a particle **aber** can be used to add emphasis;

> z.B. Das hat aber gut geschmeckt!
> That really did taste good!
>
> Das war aber dumm von dir!
> That **was** stupid of you!

8.4 ● *doch*

doch can be a one-word answer, meaning *yes*, contradicting a negative idea:

> z.B. Maria kann kein Englisch, oder? **Doch!**
> Maria can't speak English, can she? **Yes!** (= Oh yes she can!)

Used after a command form (see 10.10), **doch** can help the speaker beg or encourage the listener to go along with what he is suggesting:

> z.B. Komm doch mit!
> **Go on**, come with us!
>
> Schrei doch nicht so!
> **Please** don't shout like that!

Often **doch** shows that the speaker is protesting slightly:

> z.B. Das ist doch unmöglich!
> But that's impossible!

OR appealing for the listener to agree with him – we sometimes say *after all* for this meaning in English:

> z.B. Jan kann nicht zur Schule gehen. Er ist doch krank!
> Jan cannot go to school. After all, he's ill!

doch can also mean *nevertheless, despite everything*:

> z.B. Die Hose war sehr teuer, aber ich habe sie **doch** gekauft.
> The trousers were very expensive, but I bought them nevertheless.

8.5 ● *mal*

mal is short for **einmal**, which means *once*.

> z.B. Ich habe den Film schon **mal**/schon **einmal** gesehen.
> I've seen that film **once** already.

As a particle, it often means *just* or *just for once*. In this meaning, it is usually shortened in conversation from **einmal** to **mal**:

> Komm mal her!
> (Just) come here! (i.e. It's only a small thing I'm asking)
>
> Moment mal!
> Just a moment!
>
> Warst du schon mal in Deutschland?
> Have you ever been to Germany (once)?

nicht einmal and **nicht mal** mean *not even*:

> z.B. Die Platte kostet zwanzig Mark, aber ich habe **nicht mal/nicht einmal** zwei Mark!
> The record costs twenty Marks, but I have**n't even** got two Marks!

8.6   ● *schon*

schon means *already*, but German speakers put it into sentences much more often than we say *already* in English.

> z.B.   Es regnet schon wieder.
> It's started raining again (already).
>
> Ich verstehe schon!
> I understand! (You needn't tell me, I understand!)
>
> Das geht schon!
> It's all right!

8.7   ● *denn*

denn is often used in spoken questions, much as we use *then* in English:

> z.B.   Wie alt bist du denn?
> How old are you (then)?
>
> Was ist denn los?
> What's the matter (then)?

denn is also often used as a conjunction meaning *for* in the sense of *because* (see 9.7).

!   Do not confuse **denn** with **dann**, which means *then* in the sense of *after that* or *next*:

> z.B.   Wir deckten den Tisch. **Dann** aßen wir zu Mittag.
> We laid the table. **Then** we had lunch.

8.8   ● *zwar*

The basic meaning of **zwar** is *admittedly*:

> z.B.   Falk ist zwar ein sehr guter Schwimmer, aber Holger ist
> noch besser.
> Falk is a very good swimmer, I admit, but Holger is even better.

und zwar is used to add further details to what has already been said:

> z.B.   Wir möchten zwei Tage bleiben, **und zwar** vom fünften bis zum
> siebten Juli.
> We should like to stay for two days, from the fifth to the seventh
> of July to be precise.

word order and conjunctions

9.1 ● Word order: introduction

German word order is quite often different from English:

z.B. Nächstes Jahr besuche ich meine Freunde in Deutschland.

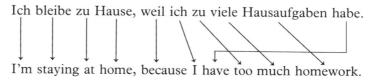

Next year I shall visit my friends in Germany.

Ich bleibe zu Hause, weil ich zu viele Hausaufgaben habe.

I'm staying at home, because I have too much homework.

The following sections explain the German system of word order.

9.2 ● Sentences and clauses

A sentence is made up of one or more *clauses*.

What is a clause?

A clause is a group of words that make sense together – normally there must be at least a subject and a verb:

z.B. Peter schwimmt.
Peter swims.

A clause can also be much longer. The first example in 9.1 above is also a sentence consisting of just one clause. However, a sentence can contain more than one clause. They may be simply added together, such as happens when **und** is put between them.

z.B. Ich mache meine Hausaufgaben, **und** meine Mutter sieht fern.
I do my homework **and** my mother watches television.

For details of this type of sentence, see 9.7.

56

9.3 ● Main clauses and subordinate clauses

In 9.2 we saw how clauses can be 'added' together to form one longer sentence. However, this is not the only way of combining clauses. Look at this example:

> Ulrike ist im Bett, weil sie krank ist.
> Ulrike is in bed because she is ill.

This sentence consists of two clauses (separated in German by the comma).

Ulrike ist im Bett is the main part of the sentence here. It could be a sentence on its own. It is the *main clause*.

weil sie krank ist is a piece of extra information joined on to the main clause. It is not a sentence in its own right. This is called a *subordinate clause*.

The subordinate clause can be joined on to the beginning of the main clause as well as on to the end.

> z.B.   Obwohl ich krank war, ging ich zur Schule.
> Although I was ill I went to school.

Here the subordinate clause is **Obwohl ich krank war**, and it comes before the main clause. For details of this type of sentence, see 9.8.

9.4 ● Word order in main clauses: the 'verb second' rule

The most important word order rule in the German language is the 'verb second' rule. According to this rule, *in a main clause, the main verb must be the second item in the clause*:

> z.B.   Ich fuhr letztes Jahr nach Österreich.
> I went to Austria last year.

The verb here is **fuhr** (*went*). In both the German and the English sentences, it is the second item. The first item is the subject **ich** (*I*). We can, however, rearrange the word order of the sentence, like this:

> Letztes Jahr **fuhr ich** nach Österreich.
> Last year **I went** to Austria.

In this version of the sentence, the first item is **Letztes Jahr** (*Last year*). Note that an 'item' can consist of more than one word. In the German sentence the verb (**fuhr**) must follow the first item immediately. The subject (**ich**) is moved, so that it comes after the verb. The English sentence has different word order: *went* is the third item, after *Last year* and *I*.

One further rearrangement of the words in this sentence is possible – in German, but not in English:

> Nach Österreich **fuhr** ich letztes Jahr.

Now, **Nach Österreich** is the first item, but the verb (**fuhr**) is still the second item.

! This word order rule is frequently broken by English speakers learning German. Do *not* say or write sentences like this:

> **X** Gestern abend, ich bin in die Disko gegangen. **X**

There should be no comma, and the sentence should read:

> Gestern abend **bin** ich in die Disko gegangen.

The first item is **Gestern abend**, then comes the verb **bin**, followed by the subject **ich**. This is a perfect tense sentence, so part of the verb is at the end – **gegangen**. This is a feature of the perfect tense (see 10.17 and following sections).

Often, there is an infinitive at the end:

> z.B.   Um sieben Uhr **muß** ich aufstehen.

Here, the main verb (**muß**) is the second item, as usual. There is also an infinitive at the end (**aufstehen**) (see 10.8).

Words or phrases which can act as the 'first item' in the main clauses

(a) The first item is very often the *subject*:

> z.B.   **Wir** gehen ins Schwimmbad.
> **We** are going to the swimming-baths.
>
> **Mein alter Deutschlehrer** hieß Smith.
> **My old German teacher** was called Smith.

(b) The first item can be the *object:*

> z.B.   **Den Briefträger** biß der Hund.
> The dog bit **the postman**.

(See 3.1 for further explanation.)

(c) The first item can also be a *time expression*:

> **Dann** kam ein Polizist an.
> **Then** a policeman arrived.
>
> **Einige Minuten später** fuhr der Zug ab.
> **A few minutes later** the train left.

There are many time expressions which can be used in this way. Some of the commonest ones are listed in 7.9.a.

(d) The first item can be some other expression. Here are a few common ones which you will need to know:

> glücklicherweise   *fortunately*
>
> unglücklicherweise   *unfortunately*
>
> leider   *unfortunately*
>
> zum Glück   *fortunately*
>
> darum   *and so, therefore*
>
> deswegen/daher   *because of this, therefore*
>
> also   *and so, therefore*

Here are some examples of these expressions in action:

> Peter lief ins Kino. **Leider** hatte der Film schon angefangen.
> Peter ran into the cinema. **Unfortunately** the film had already started.

> Wir waren sehr müde, **darum/also** gingen wir sofort nach Hause.
> We were very tired, **and so** we went home straightaway.

! English *and so* means *therefore*. It must be translated by one of the German words for *therefore*, such as **darum** or **also**. Do not use **und so**!

English *so* often means *therefore*, too, and must be treated in the same way:

> z.B. Ich mußte Geld wechseln. **Darum** ging ich zur Bank.
> I had to change some money. **So** I went to the bank.

> *All these 'first items' mean that the verb must follow immediately as the 'second item'!*

Words or phrases that cannot act as 'first item'

(a) **Ja** and **nein** at the beginning of a sentence do not count as the first item:

> z.B. **Ja**, Petra **fährt** nach München.
> **Yes**, Petra **is going** to Munich.

> **Nein**, nächste Woche **kann** ich dich nicht besuchen.
> **No**, next week I **can't** visit you.

Here, **Ja** and **Nein** do not count. The first items are **Petra** and **nächste Woche**. The verbs **fährt** and **kann** are the second items.

(b) The same thing happens with anything else placed *before a comma at the beginning*, before the main sentence starts:

> z.B. **Markus**, du **bleibst** hier, ja?
> **Markus**, you**'re staying** here, aren't you?

> **Also**, jetzt **können** wir essen!
> **Well then**, now we **can** eat!

NOTE that this last example shows a different meaning of **also** from its meaning of *therefore* described earlier in this section.

(c) **aber** meaning *however* can be placed between the first item and the verb:

> z.B. Regine ging ins Theater. **Angela aber blieb** zu Hause.
> Regine went to the theatre. **Angela, however, stayed** at home.

9.5 ● The 'time–manner–place' rule

According to this rule (often known as the 'TMP' rule), expressions of time, manner and place, when they occur next to each other in a sentence, must be placed in the order time, manner, place.

(a) Expressions of *time* include: **heute, nächste Woche**, etc. (see 7.5).

(b) Expressions of *manner* include: **schnell, mit dem Bus, zu Fuß** (expressions of manner say *how* something is done).

(c) Expressions of *place* include: **hier, dort, in die Stadt, in der Stadt**, etc.

59

Here are some sentences to show the TMP rule in action:

	time	manner	place
Ich fahre	jeden Tag	mit dem Bus	zur Schule.

I go to school by bus every day.

	time	place
Anna fährt	morgen	nach Dortmund.

Anna is going to Dortmund tomorrow.

NOTE that English puts the words in a different order!

9.6 ● The 'order of objects' rules

These are the word order rules for indirect and direct objects (for explanation of these, see 3.3. and 3.5).

Rule 1: the first rule is that, *when both objects are nouns, the indirect (dative) comes before the direct (accusative):*

	indirect object	direct object
z.B. Meine Mutter schenkte	**meinem Vater**	**einen neuen Regenschirm.**

My mother gave **my father a new umbrella**.

Rule 2: this rule says that *a pronoun comes before a noun* in the part of the sentence after the verb. This sometimes leads to the same word order as in the example above – if the pronoun represents the indirect object:

	indirect object	direct object
z.B. Meine Mutter schenkte	**ihm**	**einen neuen Regenschirm.**

My mother gave **him a new umbrella**.

But a pronoun still comes first, even if it is an accusative one that represents a direct object:

	direct object	indirect object
z.B. Meine Mutter schenkte	**ihn**	**meinem Vater.**

My mother gave **it to my father**.

Rule 3: *when both objects are pronouns, the direct object (accusative) comes first:*

	direct object	indirect object
z.B. Meine Mutter schenkte	**ihn**	**ihm.**

My mother gave **it to him**.

We can summarise these rules like this:

1 Two nouns: indirect object first
2 Pronoun and noun: pronoun first
3 Two pronouns: direct object first

9.7 ● ## Sentences made up of two main clauses 'added' together: *und, aber,* etc.

The following five conjunctions link together two main clauses, without affecting the word order in any way:

und *and*	oder *or*	denn *for* (in the sense of *because*)
aber *but*	sondern *but*	

(For the difference between **aber** and **sondern**, see (a) below.)

When these conjunctions are used, the 'verb second' rule applies to both clauses, in both halves of the sentence:

```
        verb                                      verb
       second    comma   conjunction            second
```

z.B.   Dieter hat ein Motorrad, **aber** sein Bruder hat ein Auto.
Dieter has a motor-bike, but his brother has a car.

```
      verb                               verb
     second   comma   conjunction      second
```

Heute bleiben wir in Köln **und** morgen fahren wir nach Bonn.
Today we are staying in Cologne, and tomorrow we are going to Bonn.

!   **und, oder, denn, aber** and **sondern** do not affect word order!

Points to remember

(a) **aber** is the usual word for *but*. However, **sondern** must be used when the second clause contradicts a negative statement in the first clause:

z.B.   Heute abend schen wir **nicht** fern, **sondern** wir gehen in die Disko.
Tonight we are **not** watching TV, **but** going to the disco.

Helga ist **nicht** schlank, **sondern** dick.
Helga is **not** slim **but** fat.

(b) *There must be a comma between the two clauses* EXCEPT *when* **und** *is used with the subject of the second clause omitted:*

z.B.   Katja trinkt ein Glas Cola **und** sieht fern.
Katja is having a glass of coke **and** watching TV.

This is short for:

Katja trinkt ein Glas Cola**, und sie** sieht fern.
Katja is having a glass of coke **and she** is watching TV.

• **Subordinate clauses – *Nebensätze***

Subordinate clauses are defined in 9.3.

In subordinate clauses in German, *the verb goes to the end of the clause:*

> z.B.   Ich kann nicht in Urlaub fahren, weil ich kein Geld **habe**.
> I cannot go on holiday because I have no money.

weil ich kein Geld habe is a subordinate clause, starting with the *subordinating conjunction* **weil**. The verb **habe** is moved from its usual place (ich **habe** kein Geld) to the end of the clause.

The common subordinating conjunctions which you need to know are:

weil	*because*	während	*while*
wenn	*when, if* (see 7.4)	bevor	*before* (see also 3.11)
als	*when* (one event in the past – see 7.4)	bis	*until*
		sobald	*as soon as*
daß	*that*	damit	*so that*
ob	*whether*	falls	*in case*
obwohl ⎫ obgleich ⎭ *although*		nachdem	*after* (see 10.28 and 3.11)
		seitdem	*since*

All of the above introduce subordinate clauses, in which the verb is sent to the end.

> z.B.   Ich gehe ins Kino, **wenn es** einen guten Film **gibt**.
> I go to the cinema, **when there's** a good film.
>
> Petra ging zur Fete, **obwohl/obgleich sie** viele Hausaufgaben **hatte**.
> Petra went to the party, **although she had** a lot of homework.
>
> Es ist schade, **daß du** nicht **mitkommen kannst**.
> It is a pity, **that you can't come** with us.
>
> Es war sehr spät, **als wir angekommen sind**.
> It was very late **when we arrived**.

The last two examples above show what happens when there are two verbs or when the verb is made up of more than one word:

Du **kannst** nicht mitkommen ⟶ . . . daß du nicht mitkommen **kannst**
Wir **sind** angekommen ⟶ . . . als wir angekommen **sind**

The two parts of a separable verb join together at the end of a subordinate clause (see also 10.6):

> z.B.   Vati sagt, daß ich immer zu spät **aufwache**.
> Dad says that I always **wake up** late.

Here, **aufwache** is a joined-together form of the present tense:
> Ich **wache** immer zu spät **auf**. ⟶ . . . daß ich immer spät **aufwache**.

NOTE that there must be a comma between the two clauses.

All the examples so far have shown subordinate clauses following main clauses. However, it is equally possible to have the subordinate clause first:

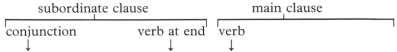

z.B. **Bevor** wir nach Hause **fahren**, **müssen** wir Geschenke kaufen.

NOTE what happens to the main clause – it starts with its verb. Whenever the subordinate clause comes before the main clause, the sentence ends up having two verbs together in the middle. In writing, there is always a comma between them.

This diagram is a summary of the word order used in sentences containing a subordinate clause:

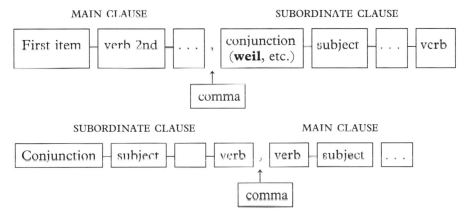

9.9 ● Relative clauses – *Relativsätze*
What is a relative clause?

A relative clause is a particular type of subordinate clause. It is a clause inserted after a noun to give further information about that noun. Here are two English examples:

> The man **who lives next door** is a policeman.
> The coat **which/that I bought** yesterday was very expensive.

The relative clauses in these two sentences give further information about *the man* and *the coat*. In English, we usually introduce relative clauses with *who*, *which* or *that*. These words are called relative pronouns. In the second example above, the *which* or *that* could even have been left out altogether:

> The coat **I bought yesterday** was very expensive.

German always requires the relative pronoun.

Relative pronouns

	m.	f.	neut.	Plural for all three genders
nom.	der	die	das	die
acc.	den	die	das	die
gen.	dessen	deren	dessen	deren
dat.	dem	der	dem	denen

Singular

Notice that most of these forms are the same as those used on the **der/die/das** marker tables (see 2.4). The ones which differ are the genitive forms, and the form for the dative plural.

How to choose the correct relative pronoun

The gender of the relative pronoun depends on the word you are referring back to:

> z.B. **Der Mann, der** nebenan wohnt, ist Polizist.
> **The man who** lives next door is a policeman.
>
> **Die Lampe, die** auf dem Tisch steht, war sehr teuer.
> **The lamp that**'s standing on the table was very expensive.

Here we have **der** referring back to **der Mann** (m.), and **die** referring back to **die Lampe** (f.). Notice that the verbs in the relative clauses (here: **wohnt**, **steht**) are at the end of those clauses. This is because relative clauses are a type of subordinate clause. In the plural, there is no problem of gender, of course:

> z.B. **Die Schuhe, die** im Schaufenster sind, sehen am schönsten aus.
> **The shoes that** are in the shop window look the nicest.

NOTE that, in German, relative clauses must be enclosed by commas.
The case of the relative pronoun depends on *the part the relative pronoun is playing inside the relative clause*. In the three examples given so far, the relative pronouns were all nominative, because they were the subjects of their clauses. We can see this, if we look at the first one again:

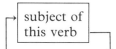

Der Mann, **der** nebenan **wohnt**, ist Polizist.

The man **who lives next door** is a policeman.

However, the relative pronoun can also be the direct object (accusative) of its clause:

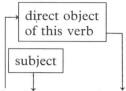

z.B.   Der Mann, **den ich** gestern **besuchte**, ist Polizist.

The man **whom I visited yesterday** is a policeman.

The underlying idea of this relative clause is *I* (subject) *visited the man* (direct object).

The dative pronouns are needed for the indirect object of the relative clause, or after prepositions requiring the dative (see 3.6):

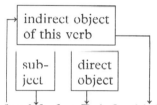

z.B.   Die Frau, **der ich den Brief schickte**, wohnt in Kiel.

The woman **to whom I sent the letter** lives in Kiel./
The woman **I sent the letter to** lives in Kiel.

(Note that we cannot imitate this last English sentence in German!)

Der Junge, **mit dem** ich Tennis spiele, heißt Jürgen.
The boy **with whom I play tennis** is called Jürgen./
The boy **I play tennis with** is called Jürgen.

In the dative plural, **denen** is needed:

Die Freunde, **mit denen** ich in Urlaub fahre, kommen aus der Schweiz.
The friends **with whom I'm going on holiday** come from Switzerland./
The friends **I'm going on holiday with** come from Switzerland.

The genitive forms **dessen** and **deren** are the German equivalents of *whose*. **dessen** refers back to a *masculine* or *neuter singular* word, and **deren** refers back to a *feminine singular* word or *any plural* word.

z.B.   Die Frau, **deren Sohn krank ist**, ist unsere Nachbarin.
The woman **whose son is ill** is our neighbour.

Der Junge, **dessen Vater im Ausland arbeitet**, wohnt bei seiner Mutter.
The boy **whose father works abroad** lives with his mother.

Remember to choose **dessen** or **deren** according to the word you are referring back to, *not* according to the word that follows.

9.10 ● **Relative clauses: *alles, was . . .*, etc.**

When referring back to something less specific than a definite noun, **was** is used to introduce the relative clause, instead of a form of **der/die/das**. This often occurs after **alles, etwas, nichts** or a superlative such as **das Beste**.

> z.B. Ich mag **alles, was** gut schmeckt.
> I like **everything that** tastes good.
>
> **Nichts, was** Peter sagt, ist interessant.
> **Nothing that** Peter says is interesting.
>
> Das ist **das Beste, was** ich für dich tun kann.
> That's **the best** (thing) **that** I can do for you.

NOTE that **was**, when used in this way, introduces a subordinate clause with the verb at the end. Note, too, that commas must be used.

9.11 ● **Two-part conjunctions: *entweder. . . oder. . .*, etc.**
(a) **entweder. . . oder. . .** means *either. . . or. . .*

> z.B. **Entweder** du machst deine Hausaufgaben, **oder** du bekommst kein Taschengeld.
> **Either** you do your homework, **or** you get no pocket-money.

NOTE that neither **entweder** nor **oder** affects word order.

(b) **weder. . . noch. . .** means *neither. . . nor. . .*

> z.B. **Weder** mein Bruder **noch** meine Schwester spielt Federball.
> **Neither** my brother **nor** my sister plays badminton.

(c) **sowohl. . . als auch. . .** means *both. . . and. . .*

> z.B. **Sowohl** meine Eltern **als auch** meine Lehrer wollen, daß ich Arzt werde.
> **Both** my parents **and** my teachers want me to become a doctor.

9.12 ● ***nicht* and word order**

nicht: introduction
nicht means *not* and is the most usual way of making a German sentence negative.

> z.B. Herr Braun arbeitet **nicht**.
> Herr Braun does **not** work.

NOTE that English often includes the verb *do* in negative sentences. This does not happen in German.

66

The German equivalent of *not a, no* and *not any* is not **nicht** but **kein** (see also 2.7).

> z.B. Das ist **kein** Problem.
> That is **not a** problem/**no** problem.
>
> Ich habe **kein** Geld.
> I have **no** money/I have**n't any** money.
>
> Ich habe **keine** Briefmarken.
> I have **no** stamps/I have**n't any** stamps.

Where to place *nicht* in the sentence

As you become more and more familiar with German, you will gradually get a 'feel' for the correct position of **nicht** in the sentence. The following rules are not the whole story, but will be of some help.

Rule 1: when there is any subject or object after the verb, **nicht** is usually left until the end (or as near as possible to the end) of the sentence.

> z.B. Ich sah den Film **nicht**.
> I did not see the film.
>
> Ich habe den Film **nicht** gesehen.
> I did not see the film
>
> Den Film habe ich **nicht** gesehen.
> I did not see the film.
>
> Schmeckt dir das Brot **nicht**?
> Don't you like the bread?

Rule 2: when the items following the verb are not subjects or objects, **nicht** usually follows the verb – i.e. the verb is second in the sentence and **nicht** is third.

> z.B. Ich bin **nicht** krank
> I am not ill.
>
> Ich gehe **nicht** in die Stadt.
> I'm not going to town.

Rule 3: when the 'time–manner–place' rule is involved (see 9.5), **nicht** usually comes before the expression of manner (if there is one) or else before the expression of place.

Ich gehe heute **nicht** zu Fuß zur Schule.
I'm not going to school on foot today.

Ich gehe heute **nicht** zur Schule.
I'm not going to school today.

Rule 4: when you want to say 'not *this*, but *this*' in German, **nicht** comes before the thing that is being ruled out.

> z.B. Ich spiele **nicht** Tennis sondern Federball.
> I'm playing not tennis but badminton.

verbs

10

10.1 ● What is a verb?

Verbs are words which usually denote an activity (e.g. *go, work, buy*), and so verbs are often labelled as 'action' words. However, some of the most frequently used verbs denote 'in-action' (e.g. *be, have, remain, stand*). No activity is going on at all: these verbs describe a static situation – a state of affairs. So, while it is convenient to think of verbs as actions, always remember that there is this other small but highly important group.

Verbs have a form called the infinitive – this is the form listed in a dictionary or vocabulary. In English the infinitive is always introduced by 'to'. In German the infinitive is just one word, ending with **-en** or **-n**:

> z.B. spiel**en**   *to play*
> arbeit**en**   *to work*
> angel**n**   *to fish*

Removing this **-en** or **-n** reveals the stem of the verb. To this stem, the various verb endings are added. We have *some* verb endings in English; for example, from the verb 'work', we have 'he work*s*' and 'I work*ed*'. German has *more* verb endings than English, however. These verb forms are explained in the following sections.

10.2 ● The present tense – *das Präsens*

The present tense describes what is happening now, or what usually happens. The German present tense corresponds to a variety of English verb forms:

> z.B. **Ich schwimme** can be translated into English as: *I swim*
> *I am swimming*
> *I do swim*

! Be careful not to use German verb forms such as „ich bin schwimmen" or „ich tue schwimmen". *I am swimming* and *I do swim* are both simply: **ich schwimme**.

10.3 • The present: regular weak verbs (regelmäßige schwache Verben)

Regular weak verbs are verbs without any peculiarities, which all have the same endings as each other. There are thousands of these verbs. We shall take as an example the verb **spielen** (to play):

ich spiel**e**	*I play, I am playing, I do play*
du spiel**st**	*you play, you are playing, you do play*
er spiel**t**	*he/it plays, etc.*
sie spiel**t**	*she/it plays, etc.*
es spiel**t**	*it plays, etc.*
wir spiel**en**	*we play, etc.*
ihr spiel**t**	*you play, etc.*
Sie spiel**en**	*you play, etc.*
sie spiel**en**	*they play, etc.*

The pronouns (**ich**, **du**, **er**, etc.) used here are explained in 4.2 to 4.4. In all verbs, in all tenses, the pronouns **er**, **sie**, and **es** share a common verb form (here, all three share the form **spielt**). This is also the form used with a singular noun subject (e.g. Meine Schwester spielt Tennis) and with **man** (meaning *one* – see 4.2.b).

In all verbs, in all tenses, the pronouns **Sie** (*you*) and **sie** (*they*) share a common verb form (here, both share the form **spielen**). This is also the form used with a plural noun subject (e.g. Meine Freunde spielen Tennis). The same verb form is also always used for **wir** (*we*).

10.4 • Verbs with a slightly irregular present tense

(a) Verbs like *arbeiten*

These are verbs in which it would be difficult to pronounce the endings **-t** and **-st** when added to the stem.

For example, **arbeiten** has the stem **arbeit-**, so **-t** cannot be added directly.

To solve this problem, **-e-** is inserted before **-st** and **-t** endings:

ich arbeite	wir arbeiten
du arbeit**e**st	ihr arbeit**e**t
er/sie/es arbeit**e**t	Sie/sie arbeiten

Other common verbs like **arbeiten** include:

warten	*to wait*	heiraten	*to get married*
reden	*to speak*	kosten	*to cost*
regnen	*to rain*	**ab**trocknen	*to dry*
antworten	*to answer*	retten	*to rescue*
baden	*to have a bath/to bathe*	zeichnen	*to draw*

(b) Verbs like *angeln*

These are verbs which have the ending **-n** where most verbs have **-en**:

ich	ang(e)le	wir	angel**n**
du	angelst	ihr	angelt
er/sie/es	angelt	Sie/sie	angel**n**

Other common verbs like **angeln** include:

wandern	*to hike*	sammeln	*to collect*
rudern	*to row*	bummeln	*to stroll*
segeln	*to sail*		

(c) Verbs in which the stem ends in an *s* sound

These verbs drop the **-s-** from the **-st** ending in the **du** part of the verb

e.g. du **heißt** (you are called), du **niest** (you sneeze),
from the verbs **heißen** and **niesen**.

10.5 ● The present: strong verbs *(starke Verben)*

Strong verbs are verbs which make alterations to their stem as well as adding the normal endings. As an example, here is the verb **sprechen** (*to speak*):

ich	spreche	wir	sprechen
du	spr**i**chst	ihr	sprecht [⚠ No change here]
er/sie/es	spr**i**cht	Sie/sie	sprechen

Sprechen changes **e** to **i** in the **du** and **er/sie/es** parts. Other strong verbs make a variety of different changes, but the parts of the verb which are affected are always the same: **du** and **er/sie/es**.

Other examples in brief form:

fahren:	du f**ä**hrst, er/sie/es f**ä**hrt	*to go, to drive*
sehen:	du s**ie**hst, er/sie/es s**ie**ht	*to see*
nehmen:	du n**imm**st, er/sie/es n**imm**t	*to take*
laufen:	du l**äu**fst, er/sie/es l**äu**ft	*to run/walk*

There are many strong verbs. You can find them in the Verb list (10.43).

Strong verbs with slight peculiarities

These verbs have shortened the normal endings:

lesen:	du **liest**, er/sie/es liest	*to read*
essen:	du **ißt**, er/sie/es ißt	*to eat (fressen and vergessen* are similar)
halten:	du hältst, er/sie/es **hält**	*to hold, to stop*
treten:	du trittst, er/sie/es **tritt**	*to step, to kick*
einladen:	du lädst ein, er/sie/es **lädt** ein	*to invite*

(For more on strong verbs, see 10.14 and 10.21.)

10.6 ● Separable verbs (trennbare Verben) – all tenses

(a) These are verbs which consist of two parts: a *basic verb*, plus a *prefix*. We have something like this in English:

z.B.   I **switched** the light **off**.
       I often **go out** in the evenings.

In English, the two parts of the verb are always separated. In German, they are sometimes separated and sometimes together. Here are some examples based on the separable verb **aufmachen** (*to open*):

Ich kann die Tür nicht **aufmachen.** ⟵   *infinitive:* joined together
I can't open the door.

Ich **mache** die Tür **auf.** ⟵   *present tense:* separated
I am opening the door.

Ich **machte** die Tür **auf.** ⟵   *simple past tense:* separated
I opened the door.   (see 10.13)

Ich **habe** die Tür **aufgemacht.** ⟵   *perfect tense:* joined together
I opened the door.   (see 10.17)

Vati weiß, daß ich die Tür **aufmache.** ⟵   *subordinate clause:* joined
Dad knows that I'm opening the door.   (see 9.8)   together

(b) How to use *hin* and *her*

These two words usually form themselves into separable verb prefixes, such as **hin**gehen, **her**kommen, etc.

The basic idea behind **hin** is going away,
and   the basic idea behind **her** is coming towards.

Used on their own **hin** is short for **dorthin** and means *(to) there*
and **her** is short for **hierher** and means *(to) here*:

z.B.   Morgen gehen wir **hin.**   Komm **her**!
       Tomorrow we'll go there.   Come here!

       Wollen wir **hin**gehen?   Du sollst **her**kommen!
       Shall we go there?   You're to come here!

hin can also mean down, as in the verbs **hin**legen and **hin**stellen (*to put something down*).

Very often, **hin** and **her** are combined into longer prefixes, such as:

hinein-/herein-   *in*
hinaus-/heraus-   *out*
hinauf-/herauf-   *up*
hinunter-/herunter-   *down*
hinab-/herab-   *down*

Here are some examples of these in use:

z.B.   Komm **herein**!   Wir gingen zur Burg **hinauf.**
       Come **in**!   We went **up** to the castle.

       Wollen wir **hinein**gehen? Wir gingen ins Tal **hinab/hinunter.**
       Shall we go **in**?   We went **down** into the valley.

These prefixes are often used to strengthen what has, in fact, already been said:

> z.B. Ich ging **in die Stadt hinein.** Er kam **aus dem Haus heraus.**
> I went **into the town.** He came **out of the house.**

To say *up the hill* or *down the street*, the relevant noun is put into the accusative:

> z.B. Ich ging **den Berg hinauf.**
> I went **up the mountain.**
>
> Ich ging **die Straße hinunter/hinab.**
> I went **down the street/road.**

In conversation (especially in Northern Germany), the **hin-** forms of these prefixes are not much used. The **her-** forms are used instead, often with the **her-** shortened to simply **'r-**:

> z.B. Ich ging **in die Stadt 'rein.** Ich ging **die Straße 'runter.**
> I went **into the town.** I went **down the street/road.**

10.7 ● The present: reflexive verbs *(reflexive Verben)*

These are verbs in which the subject and direct object are the same person or thing – i.e. the subject does something to himself/herself/itself. Here, as an example, is the present tense of **sich wiegen** (*to weigh oneself*):

ich	wiege **mich**		wir	wiegen **uns**
du	wiegst **dich**		ihr	wiegt **euch**
er/sie/es	wiegt **sich**		Sie/sie	wiegen **sich**

Ich wiege mich means *I weigh myself*, **du wiegst dich** means *you weigh yourself*, etc. The words **mich, dich, sich**, etc. are known as *reflexive pronouns*.

! NOTE the word order used to form a question: **Wiegst du dich?**

(a) Common reflexive verbs

There are quite a few of these in German. Many of them are verbs whose English equivalents do not involve *myself, yourself*, etc. Here is a useful selection:

sich **ab**trocknen	*to dry oneself*	sich erkälten	*to catch a cold*
sich **an**ziehen	*to get dressed*	sich freuen	*to be pleased*
sich **aus**ziehen	*to get undressed*	sich **hin**legen	*to lie down*
sich **um**ziehen	*to get changed*	sich **hin**setzen	*to sit down*
sich ärgern	*to get annoyed*	sich kämmen	*to comb one's hair*
sich **aus**ruhen	*to have a rest*	sich rasieren	*to have a shave*
sich beeilen	*to hurry up*	sich schminken	*to put make-up on*
sich entschuldigen	*to apologise*	sich treffen (see 12.3)	*to meet (each other)*
sich erinnern... ...an + acc.	*to remember*	sich waschen	*to have a wash*

(For the perfect tense of reflexive verbs, see 10.25.)

(b) Expressions with the reflexive pronoun in the dative

!

When a person does something for his or her own benefit, German often uses the formula: verb + dative reflexive pronoun + a direct object (acc.) Many of these verbs are connected with the idea of *looking after oneself*. A typical example is **sich die Hände waschen** (*to wash one's hands*):

ich wasche **mir** die Hände	wir waschen **uns** die Hände
du wäschst **dir** die Hände	ihr wascht **euch** die Hände
er/sie/es wäscht **sich** die Hände	Sie/sie waschen **sich** die Hände

Notice these dative reflexive pronouns. Most of them are the same as the ordinary accusative reflexive pronouns shown earlier in this section, but **mich** has become **mir**, and **dich** has become **dir**.

Here are some examples of the same expression in other contexts and tenses:

Ich muß mir die Hände waschen.
I must wash my hands.

Dann wusch ich mir die Hände.
Then I washed my hands.

Ich habe mir die Hände gewaschen.
I washed my hands.

Other similar expressions are:

sich die Zähne/Schuhe putzen	*to clean one's teeth/shoes*
sich etwas **an**sehen	*to have a look at something*
sich etwas kaufen	*to buy oneself something*
sich etwas **aus**suchen	*to find oneself something*

(c) To have something done for oneself – using *lassen*

To say that you have/get something done for yourself (e.g. *have your hair cut*), use **lassen** with an infinitive (see also 10.32.a). This often involves a dative reflexive pronoun, as in these examples:

Sie läßt sich die Haare schneiden.
She is having her hair cut.

Schmidts lassen sich ein Haus bauen.
The Schmidts are having (themselves) a house built.

(For the perfect tense of **lassen** + *infinitive*, see 10.27.)

10.8 ● The present: modal verbs *(Modalverben)*

These are six verbs which are very commonly used in German. They are irregular, and their present tenses are therefore set out in full below. They are mostly used with another verb, which is always in the infinitive form and at the end (or as near as possible to the end) of the clause or sentence. A few examples only are given here. Many more can be found in section 12.

können ('can, to be able to')

ich kann [no **e** ending]	wir können
du kannst	ihr könnt
er/sie/es kann [no **t** ending]	Sie/sie können

z.B. Was **kann** ich für dich **tun**?
What **can** I **do** for you?

Leider **können** wir nicht **mitkommen**.
Unfortunately we **can**'t **come** with you.

NOTE that the infinitives **tun** and **mitkommen** come at the end of these examples. For other examples, see 12.2.

müssen ('must, to have to')

ich muß [no **e** ending]	wir müssen
du mußt	ihr müßt
er/sie/es muß [no **t** ending]	Sie/sie müssen

z.B. Du **mußt** deine Hausaufgaben **machen**.
You **must do** your homework.

! NOTE: **müssen** + **nicht** = *don't have to*.

z.B. Du **mußt nicht rauchen**.
You **don't have to smoke**.

This does *not* mean 'You *mustn't* smoke', which is expressed using **dürfen** (see below).

wollen ('to want to')

ich will [no **e** ending]	wir wollen
du willst	ihr wollt
er/sie/es will [no **t** ending]	Sie/sie wollen

! This verb means *want to*. It is *not* the equivalent of *will* in English and is *not* used to form the future tense! (For the future, see 10.29.)

> z.B. Susanne **will** ein neues Kleid **kaufen**.
> Susanne **wants to buy** a new dress.

NOTE that **wollen wir?** is used for *shall we?*

> z.B. **Wollen wir** ein Eis kaufen?
> **Shall we** buy an ice-cream?

(See also 10.41.b.)

---

sollen ('to be supposed to, to be meant to, to be due to')

ich soll [no **e** ending]	wir sollen
du sollst	ihr sollt
er/sie/es soll [no **t** ending]	Sie/sie sollen

This verb has many English equivalents. Often we say *shall* (as in: *What shall I do?* meaning *What am I supposed to do?*), but **sollen** has nothing to do with the future tense and is not used for *shall* in sentences such as *I shall go to London tomorrow.* (For the future, see 10.29.) Basically, **sollen** has a meaning which is a weaker version of **müssen**. **Müssen** says what *must be done*, **sollen** says what *is supposed to be done*.

> z.B. Wann **soll** ich **zurücksein?**
> When **shall I be back?**/ When **am I supposed to be back?**
>
> **Soll** ich dir **helfen?**   Er **soll** krank **sein**.
> **Shall I help** you?   He's **supposed to be** ill.

There is also a special form of **sollen**, which means *ought to* or *should*. This is **sollte**. Here is an example.

> Du bist doch krank. Du **solltest** zum Arzt gehen.
> You're ill. You **ought to/should** go to the doctor's.

---

dürfen ('may, to be allowed to')

ich darf [no **e** ending]	wir dürfen
du darfst	ihr dürft
er/sie/es darf [no **t** ending]	Sie/sie dürfen

This verb is about having *permission* to do things:

> z.B. Ich **darf** nicht **schwimmen gehen**.
> I'm not **allowed to go swimming**.
>
> In der Schule **darf** man nicht **essen**.
> You're not **allowed to eat** in school.

When asking for permission, **darf ich?** is more polite than **kann ich?**:

> z.B. **Darf** ich ins Kino **gehen?**   **Kann** ich ins Kino **gehen?**
> **May** I **go** to the cinema?   **Can** I **go** to the cinema?

75

!	**Dürfen** + **nicht** is often the equivalent of English *must not*:

z.B. Das **darfst** du **nicht machen**.
    You **mustn't do** that. (= You**'re not allowed to do** that.)

REMEMBER that **müssen** + **nicht** means *don't have to*, not *mustn't* (see above).

---

mögen ('to like')

ich mag [no **e** ending]	wir mögen
du magst	ihr mögt
er/sie/es mag [no **t** ending]	Sie/sie mögen

This verb is different from the other modals, since it is mostly used without another verb in the infinitive. It means *like*, and is especially used for *liking* foods and people:

z.B. Ich **mag** ihn (gern).
    I **like** him.

    Ich **mag** ihn **nicht**.
    I **don't like** him.

    Tomaten **mag** ich **sehr gern**.
    I **really like** tomatoes.

Bananen **mag** ich **nicht so gern**.
I**'m not keen on** bananas.

Ich **mag keine** Apfelsinen.
I **don't like** oranges.

!	The most common form of **mögen** is not the present tense, but **möchte** (*would like*), which is especially useful when shopping:

z.B. **Ich möchte** bitte ein Kilo Birnen.
    I'd like a kilo of pears, please.

Leaving out the second verb after a modal verb
This is never compulsory, but it is often done in spoken German. In these examples, the verb in brackets could easily be left out because the verb intended is obvious:

z.B. Ich muß zum Arzt (gehen).
    I must go to the doctor's.

    Ich will nach Berlin (fahren).
    I want to go to Berlin.

    Udo kann sehr gut Englisch (sprechen).
    Udo can speak English very well.

    Ich kann nicht mit(kommen).
    I can't come with you.

gehen and **fahren** are the verbs most often left out.

(Other tenses of modal verbs are described in 10.15 and 10.27.)

10.9 ● The present: *sein, haben, werden, wissen*

Apart from the modals there are four verbs which have an irregular present tense:

sein *to be*	werden *to become*
haben *to have*	wissen *to know*

sein ('to be')

ich **bin**	wir **sind**
du **bist**	ihr **seid**
er/sie/es **ist**	Sie/sie **sind**

This verb is also irregular in English: *I am, you are, he is*, etc.

Here is an example of **sein** in use:

Wie alt **bist du**, Robert?   **Ich bin** sechzehn Jahre alt.
How old **are you**, Robert?   **I am** sixteen years old.

sein is also used to help form the perfect tense of some verbs (see 10.22).

haben ('to have')

ich **habe**	wir **haben**
du **hast**	ihr **habt**
er/sie/es **hat**	Sie/sie **haben**

z.B.   **Hast du** Geschwister?   Ja, **ich habe** zwei Schwestern.
       Have you any brothers or   Yes, **I have** two sisters.
       sisters?

haben is also used to help form the perfect tense of most verbs (see 10.17 onwards).

In some expressions, German has **haben** where English has the verb *to be*.

z.B.   **Ich habe** Hunger/Durst.   **Ich habe** recht/unrecht.
       I am hungry/thirsty.   **I am** right/wrong.

werden ('to become')

ich **werde**	wir **werden**
du **wirst**	ihr **werdet**
er/sie/es **wird**	Sie/sie **werden**

In English, we use a number of different verbs to convey the meaning *become*. These are all expressed by **werden** in German:

z.B.   Ich **werde** müde.   Ilse **wird** oft krank.
       I'm **becoming/getting/growing** tired.   Ilse often **falls** ill.

werden is also used to help form the future tense (see 10.29) and the passive (see 10.34).

wissen ('to know')

ich **weiß** [no **e** ending]	wir **wissen**
du **weißt**	ihr **wißt**
er/sie/es **weiß** [no **t** ending]	Sie/sie **wissen**

This verb is used to mean *know* in the sense of knowing information. It is *not* used to mean *know* in the sense of *be acquainted with* (which is **kennen**). For more on this, see 10.42.

z.B. **Weißt du**, wo der Bahnhof ist?   Nein, **das weiß ich nicht.**
Do you know where the station is?   No, **I don't know (that).**

In conversation, **das weiß ich nicht** is often shortened to **weiß ich nicht**.

10.10 ● Commands, instructions and suggestions

We use command forms to get people to do things (see also 12.3). Command forms are not necessarily used for ordering people about. They can be polite requests. For example, **entschuldigen Sie, bitte** (*excuse me, please*) is a command form, but it is also polite. In German, command forms vary depending on the person you are talking to. These are described below. The difference between **du**, **ihr** and **Sie** is treated in 4.3.

(a) Commands to use when talking to someone you address as *du*

Basic rule: take the **du** part of the present tense, and remove the word **du** and the **-st** ending:

z.B. du spielst ⟶ **spiel!**   *play!*   (from the verb **spielen**)
     du gibst ⟶ **gib!**   *give!*   (from the verb **geben**)
     du sprichst ⟶ **sprich!**   *speak!*   (from the verb **sprechen**)

This means that strong verbs (like **sprechen** – see 10.5) keep the change made in their stem in the **du** part.

EXCEPTION: with strong verbs Umlaut is added in the **du** part but is dropped in the command:

z.B.   du fährst ⟶ **fahr!**   *go!*   (from the verb **fahren**)
     du schläfst ⟶ **schlaf!**   *sleep!*   (from the verb **schlafen**)
     du läufst ⟶ **lauf!**   *run!*   (from the verb **laufen**)
NOTE: **du ißt** ⟶ **iß!** (*eat!*); and **du liest** ⟶ **lies!** (*read!*)

Sometimes, **du** commands are given the ending **-e**. This is usually optional, and in spoken German the **-e** is mostly left off. Here are some command forms showing the **-e** ending:

singe! OR sing!   *sing!*

schwimme! OR schwimm!   *swim!*

However, some strong verbs cannot have the **-e** ending:

> iß! *eat!*
> nimm! *take!*

So it is usually safest to leave off the **-e** ending. Two small groups of verbs must have the **-e** ending, however. These are the verbs like **arbeiten** and **angeln** (see 10.4). The only correct forms here are:

> arbeite! *work!*
> ang(e)le! *fish!*

entschuldigen (*to excuse*) has the form **entschuldige!** (*excuse me!*)

sein (*to be*) has an irregular command form: **sei!**

> z.B. **Sei** still! *Be quiet!*

(b) Commands to use when talking to people you address as *ihr*

Rule: take the **ihr** part of the present tense and remove the word **ihr**:

> ihr schwimmt ⟶ **schwimmt!** *swim!*
> ihr schlaft ⟶ **schlaft!** *sleep!*
> ihr lauft ⟶ **lauft!** *run!*
> ihr arbeitet ⟶ **arbeitet!** *work!*
> ihr seid ⟶ **seid (still)!** *be (quiet)!*

(c) Commands to use when talking to people you address as *Sie*

Rule: take the **Sie** part of the present tense and turn the words around.

> z.B. Sie schwimmen ⟶ **schwimmen Sie!** *swim!*
> Sie schlafen ⟶ **schlafen Sie!** *sleep!*

For **sein** (*to be*), the form is **seien Sie!**:

> z.B. **Seien Sie** still! *Be quiet!*

(d) 'To whom it may concern!' – commands and instructions

In this kind of an instruction – to anyone it may concern – the infinitive is used. Instructions like these are especially common in written German, in recipes, in directions for use, and in public notices and signs.

> z.B. **Aufmachen!**
> Open up! (i.e. open the door)
>
> Nicht **schießen!**
> No shooting!
>
> Bitte sofort **anrufen.**
> Please telephone at once.
>
> Die Schnitzel **klopfen, salzen** und **pfeffern.**
> Beat the schnitzels to flatten them out, then season with salt and pepper.

(e) 'Let's . . .' (suggestion)

z.B. wir tanzen   ⟶ **tanzen wir!**   *let's dance*

wir fangen an   ⟶ **fangen wir an!**   *let's start*

For **sein** the form is **seien wir**

z.B. **seien wir vorsichtig!** *let's be careful*

(See also 12.3.)

NOTE that there are two other ways of expressing *let's* in German:

z.B. Wir wollen tanzen! *Let's dance!*
Lassen Sie uns gehen! *Let's go!*

10.11 ● The present participle: German and English compared

In German this verb form is made by adding **-d** to the infinitive.
German present participles are used as adjectives, with adjective endings.
The corresponding English word usually ends in *-ing*.

z.B. aufregen *to excite* ⟶ **aufregend**: Das war ein **aufregender** Film.
                                          That was an **exciting** film.

lächeln *to smile* ⟶ **lächelnd**: sein **lächelndes** Gesicht
                                            his **smiling** face

And, like adjectives, present participles can also be used as adverbs:

z.B. „Guten Tag", sagte sie **lächelnd**.
'Hello', she said, **smiling(ly)**.

!

Despite these examples, English forms ending in *-ing* cannot usually be translated by German present participles. In sentences like the following one, a clause is usually needed instead:

Arriving at the station, I bought a ticket.
Als ich am Bahnhof ankam, kaufte ich eine Fahrkarte.
(= When I arrived at the station, I bought a ticket.)

In other contexts, other solutions may be needed:

z.B. We enjoyed **playing football**.
Es hat uns Spaß gemacht, **Fußball zu spielen**.
(= It was fun for us to play football.)

10.12 ● The simple past tense – *das Präteritum*

You need this tense to talk about the past. It is called 'simple' because the verb consists of just one word. The simple past has many other names. Some people call it the *imperfect*, others the *preterite*. In German, it is usually called **das Präteritum**.

The simple past corresponds to a variety of English past tenses, for example:

Ich spielte can be translated into English as:
I played, I used to play, I was playing, I did play

| ! | Be careful not to invent German past tense forms such as „ich war spielen". This is not the German past tense! *I was playing* is simply: **ich spielte**. |

10.13 ● The simple past: regular and slightly irregular weak verbs

There are thousands of verbs which follow the pattern of:

spielen ('to play')

ich spiel**te**	wir spiel**ten**
du spiel**test**	ihr spiel**tet**
er/sie/es spiel**te** [no **t** ending]	Sie/sie spiel**ten**

Examples of this tense in action:

Gestern **spielte ich** Federball.
Yesterday **I played** badminton.

Als Kind **spielte ich** Fußball.
As a child, **I played/used to play** football.

Ich spielte Karten, als sie kam.
I was playing cards when she came.

Verbs with a slightly irregular simple past
Verbs like **arbeiten** (see 10.4) have an **-e-** before the **-te** endings:

z.B. ich arbeit**e**te, du arbeit**e**test, er arbeit**e**te, etc.

10.14 ● The simple past: strong verbs *(starke Verben)*

We have strong verbs in the English simple past tense:

z.B. I sing ⟶ I sang, I write ⟶ I wrote, I drive ⟶ I drove

The German strong verbs behave in a similar way: they change their stem in the simple past. The endings they use are as shown in the example verb:

singen ('to sing')

ich sang [no **e** ending]	wir sang**en**
du sang**st**	ihr sang**t**
er/sie/es sang [no **t** ending]	Sie/sie sang**en**

There are many other strong verbs besides **singen**. They can be found in the Verb list (10.43).

⚿ 10.15 ● The simple past: modal verbs *(Modalverben)*

In the simple past, the six modal verbs (see 10.8) have the **-te** endings of regular weak verbs (as in 10.13), but some of them make a slight alteration to their stem as well:

können ⟶	ich **konnte**	*I could, was able to*
müssen ⟶	ich **mußte**	*I had to*
wollen ⟶	ich **wollte**	*I wanted to*
sollen ⟶	ich **sollte**	*I was to, was supposed to*
dürfen ⟶	ich **durfte**	*I was allowed to*
mögen ⟶	ich **mochte**	*I liked*

NOTE that the modals which have Umlaut in the infinitive all lose the Umlaut in the simple past. Here are examples of three of them in use:

Leider **konnte** ich gestern nicht kommen.
Unfortunately I **couldn't** (**was not able to**) come yesterday.

Ich **mußte** nach London fahren.
I **had to** go to London.

Ich **sollte** zur Bank gehen.
I **was supposed to** go to the bank.

10.16 ● The simple past: irregular verbs

There are a few verbs with an irregular simple past, and they are shown here. Most of them combine a change in their stem with the **-te** endings of weak verbs. Because of this, they are often known as *mixed* verbs.

haben	*to have* ⟶	ich **hatte**	
kennen	*to know* ⟶	ich **kannte**	
wissen	*to know* ⟶	ich **wußte**	
bringen	*to bring* ⟶	ich **brachte**	
verbringen	*to spend time* ⟶	ich **verbrachte**	
denken	*to think* ⟶	ich **dachte**	
rennen	*to run* ⟶	ich **rannte**	
nennen	*to name* ⟶	ich **nannte**	
brennen	*to burn* ⟶	ich **brannte**	(also: **verbrennen**)

(For the difference between **kennen** and **wissen**, see 10.42.)

The most irregular is **werden** (*to become*). It has endings in **-de** instead of **-te**:

ich **wurde**	wir **wurden**
du **wurdest**	ihr **wurdet**
er/sie/es **wurde**	Sie/sie **wurden**

! **sein** (*to be*) is *not* irregular in the simple past. It is like a strong verb, and has the simple past ich **war**, du **warst**, er/sie/es **war**, etc.

10.17 ● The perfect tense – *das Perfekt*

Apart from the simple past tense (described in the last five sections above), German has another major past tense. This is the perfect. It is made up of two elements: the present tense of either **haben** or **sein** (see 10.22) *plus* a special verb form called the *past participle*:

Ich **habe** Tischtennis **gespielt**.

I **played** table-tennis.

Ich **bin** mit dem Auto **gefahren**.

I **went** by car.

NOTE that the past participle is placed at the end of the clause.

Like other German tenses, the perfect corresponds to a variety of English tenses. For example:

Ich habe gespielt can be translated as:
I played, I have played, I used to play, I did play

10.18 ● The perfect and the simple past compared

There is for all practical purposes no real difference between the simple past and the perfect, although there are variations in usage. If you compare the English translations given for **Ich spielte** in 10.12 and for **Ich habe gespielt** in 10.17 above, you will see that they are largely identical.

In spoken German, both tenses are used, but there is a tendency to prefer the perfect. In South Germany, Switzerland and Austria, the simple past is very little used in speech – the perfect is used instead. As an English-speaking learner of German, you can use either tense when speaking about the past. You can treat the two tenses as interchangeable.

! *In written German, the simple past is the main tense to use.* When writing a past tense story, you *must* use the simple past. In letter-writing, both tenses are equally acceptable.

10.19 ● The perfect: regular and slightly irregular weak verbs that take *haben*

The tense is constructed by using the present tense of **haben** (see 10.9) *plus* a past participle. This is made by taking the stem of the verb and putting **ge-** as a prefix before it and **-t** on the end of it.

z.B.　spielen　*to play*　⟶　**ge**spiel**t**
　　　tanzen　*to dance*　⟶　**ge**tanz**t**
　　　zahlen　*to pay*　⟶　**ge**zahl**t**

The past participle is placed at the end (or as near as possible to the end) of the clause or sentence:

z.B. Gestern **habe ich** Tennis **gespielt**.
Yesterday **I played** tennis.

Dann **haben wir** in der Disko **getanzt**.
Then **we danced** at the disco.

Wir haben zehn Mark **gezahlt**.
We paid ten Marks.

In subordinate clauses (see 9.8), the word order is like this:

Heute bin ich müde, weil **ich** Tennis **gespielt habe**.
Today I am tired, because **I played** tennis.

Verbs with a slightly irregular past participle
Verbs like **arbeiten** (see 10.4) have **-et**
instead of **-t** on the end of the past participle:

Ich habe im Garten gearbeit**et**.
I worked in the garden.

10.20 ● **The perfect: verbs with an inseparable prefix**

Some verbs have an inseparable prefix (i.e. a prefix which never separates from the verb). They make their past participles without adding **ge-**.

z.B. besuchen *to visit* ⟶ Ich habe meinen Onkel **besucht**.
I visited my uncle.

┌─────────────────────────────┐
│ past participles without **ge-** │
└─────────────────────────────┘

verkaufen *to sell* ⟶ Ich habe mein Fahrrad **verkauft**.
I sold my bicycle.

Some typical inseparable verbs are:

erzählen *to tell*	empfehlen *to recommend*
entschuldigen *to excuse*	mißverstehen *to misunderstand*
zerbrechen *to smash*	gefallen *to please*

NOTE that the last four of these are strong verbs (see 10.21).

10.21 ● **The perfect: strong verbs** *(starke Verben)*

The past participles of strong verbs can be found in the Verb list (10.43). They start with **ge-** (or with one of the inseparable prefixes given in 10.20), but they end in **-en**, instead of the **-t** used with weak verbs. Here are a few examples:

schreiben *to write* → Ich habe einen Brief **ge**schrieb**en**.
I wrote a letter.

trinken *to drink* → Wir haben Bier **ge**trunk**en**.
We drank beer.

beginnen *to begin* → Der Film hat gerade **be**gonn**en**.
The film has just begun.

For more on strong verbs see 10.5 and 10.14.

84

10.22 ● **The perfect: with *haben* or *sein*?**

Although the great majority of verbs form the perfect tense with **haben**, some take **sein** instead. The verbs concerned may be weak, strong, inseparable, separable, or any other type! So how do you tell which verbs take **sein**?

Rule 1: All verbs which have, or usually have, a direct object must take **haben**. These are traditionally known as transitive verbs. An example is **trinken**. You normally drink *something* (a direct object), so **trinken** takes **haben**: **ich habe Apfelsaft getrunken.**

Rule 2: Verbs without a direct object (intransitive verbs) also take **haben**, except for:

(a) Verbs denoting *motion* from place to place. These take **sein**.

z.B. gehen → Ich **bin** zu Fuß **gegangen**.
I went on foot.

fahren → Ulli **ist** nach Ulm **gefahren**.
Ulli went to Ulm.

fliegen → Ich **bin** nach Amerika **geflogen**.
I flew to America.

(b) Verbs denoting a *change of state*. These also take **sein**. For example:

z.B. aufwachen → Ich **bin** früh **aufgewacht**.
I woke up early.

sterben → Mein Hund **ist** 1983 **gestorben**.
My dog died in 1983.

werden → Helga **ist** reich **geworden**.
Helga became/got rich.

(c) Some other verbs. These two are the most important:
sein → Ich **bin** in Urlaub **gewesen**.
I was on holiday.

bleiben → Karin **ist** zu Hause **geblieben**.
Karin stayed at home.

Verbs which can take *haben* or *sein*

(d) Verbs denoting motion, such as **schwimmen** (*to swim*), **segeln** (*to sail*) and **rudern** (*to row*), sometimes take **haben** when they show *motion within one place* (i.e. not motion *from* place *to* place):

z.B. Ich **habe** im Fluß **geschwommen**.
I swam in the river.

But **sein** is never wrong with these verbs. We can also say:

Ich **bin** im Fluß **geschwommen**.
I swam in the river.

For English-speaking learners of German, it is safer to stick to **sein** with these verbs.

(e) Some verbs which have two different meanings need **sein** for one meaning and **haben** for the other. The main example of this that you are likely to meet is **fahren**. It normally means *go* and takes **sein**:

> z.B.   Gestern **sind** wir nach Wien **gefahren**.
> Yesterday we **went** to Vienna.

However, **fahren** can also mean *drive*, as in *drive someone to a place*. In this meaning, it has a direct object. Under 'Rule 1' above, verbs with a direct object must take **haben**:

> Meine Mutter **hat mich** zum Bahnhof **gefahren**.
> My mother **drove me** to the station.

There are rare exceptions to some of the rules in this section, but the rules given here will cover virtually all the verbs you are likely to need.

10.23 ● The perfect: verbs ending in *-ieren*

These verbs are weak verbs, but they do *not* have the prefix **ge-** in their past participles:

> z.B.   telefonieren ⟶ Ich **habe** mit Hans **telefoniert**.
> I spoke to Hans on the phone.
>
> reparieren ⟶ Ich **habe** mein Fahrrad **repariert**.
> I repaired my bike.

10.24 ● The perfect: separable verbs *(trennbare Verben)*

Separable verbs have **-ge-** sandwiched in the middle of their past participles. Here are examples for both weak and strong verbs:

> **auf**wachen ⟶ Ich bin um sieben Uhr auf**ge**wacht.
> I woke up at 7 o'clock.
>
> **aus**ziehen ⟶ Ich habe meinen Mantel aus**ge**zogen.
> I took off my coat.

10.25 ● The perfect: reflexive verbs *(reflexive Verben)*

These all take **haben** in German:

> z.B.   sich anziehen ⟶ Ich **habe mich** schnell **angezogen**.
> I got dressed quickly.

10.26 ● The perfect: irregular verbs *(unregelmäßige Verben)*

These verbs have an irregular past participle. They can be found in the Verb list (10.43). These same verbs were also dealt with in 10.16.

> z.B.   bringen ⟶ Dieter hat uns zum Bahnhof **gebracht**.
> Dieter took us to the station.

10.27 ● The perfect: modal verbs (Modalverben)

Modal verbs are not often used in the perfect tense – the simple past is normally used instead – so they will be described here very briefly. Modals are almost always used with another verb. In the perfect, this other verb is the next-to-last word in the clause or sentence. The final word is the modal verb itself – *in the infinitive*. **haben** (never **sein**) is used.

> z.B. Ich **habe** dich gestern nicht **besuchen können**.
> I couldn't visit you yesterday.
>
> Ich **habe** nach Berlin **fahren müssen**.
> I had to go to Berlin.

When the modal verb is used without another verb, there are special past participles: **gekonnt, gemußt, gewollt, gesollt, gedurft** and **gemocht**. These are rare, except in the phrase:
Das habe ich nicht gewollt (*I didn't mean to*).

lassen + infinitive (see 10.7.c) forms its perfect tense in the same way:

> z.B. Ich **habe** mir die Haare **schneiden lassen**.
> I have had my hair cut.

10.28 ● The pluperfect tense – *das Plusquamperfekt*

In English, this tense is made up of *had* and a past participle. For example: 'I *had* never *seen* that film before'. The pluperfect usually denotes an event further back in the past than other past tenses.

> e.g. After I **had bought** some bread, I **went** home.

In this example, the pluperfect shows that the buying of the bread took place further back in the past than the going home.

In German, the pluperfect is constructed in a very similar way to the perfect tense. The only difference is that the present tenses of **haben** and **sein** are replaced by their simple past forms (see 10.16). This means that we use: **hatte** (or **war** for verbs which take **sein**) *plus* the past participle.

> z.B. Ich **hatte** den Film noch nie **gesehen**.
> I had never seen that film before.
>
> Ich **war** schon 1982 in Rom **gewesen**.
> I had already been to Rome in 1982.

You will most often need to use the pluperfect in subordinate clauses beginning with **nachdem** (*after*).

> z.B. Nachdem **ich** Brot **gekauft hatte**, ging ich nach Hause.
> After **I had bought** some bread, I went home.
>
> Nachdem **wir** nach New York **geflogen waren**, fuhren wir mit dem Zug nach Washington.
> After **we had flown** to New York, we went by train to Washington.

● **Referring to the future**

German has a future tense which consists of the present tense of **werden** (see 10.9) *plus* an infinitive (which is sent to the end of the sentence).

> z.B. Ich **werde** eines Tages **heiraten**.
> I **shall get married** one day.

However, this future tense is not very often used. Whenever it is already clear that you are talking about the future, you can simply use the present tense:

> z.B. Ich fahre jetzt in die Stadt, aber **ich bin** um vier Uhr wieder hier.
> I am going into town now, but I **shall be** back here at four o'clock.
>
> Morgen **gehen wir** schwimmen.
> Tomorrow **we'll go** swimming.

For more ways of talking about the future, see 12.3.

10.30 ● **The dative used with verbs**

German has many verbs and verbal expressions which involve the use of the dative. The main ones are explained below. (For basic general information on the dative, see 3.5.)

(a) Verbs with a dative object

With these verbs the object is in the dative (where you would have expected to find an accusative direct object). Here is a useful list:

verzeihen + dat.	*to pardon, excuse*	vergeben + dat.	*to forgive*
begegnen★ + dat.	*to meet by chance*	helfen + dat.	*to help*
antworten + dat.	*to answer someone*	danken + dat.	*to thank*
glauben + dat.	*to believe someone*	gehören + dat.	*to belong to*
verbieten + dat.	*to forbid someone to. . .*	folgen★ + dat.	*to follow*
sich nähern + dat.	*to approach*	erlauben + dat.	*to allow*

★The asterisked verbs form the perfect tense with **sein**.

> z.B. Kannst du **mir** helfen?
> Can you help me?
>
> Ich dankte **dem Gepäckträger**.
> I thanked the porter.
>
> Der Polizist folgte **dem Dieb**.
> The policeman followed the thief.
>
> Peter antwortete **ihr** nicht.
> Peter did not answer her.
>
> Wir näherten uns **der Berghütte**.
> We approached the mountain hut.

(b) gefallen

gefallen is often used in sentences where we would say *like* in English. However, the German sentence is the opposite way round from the English equivalent.

z.B.   Der Pullover gefällt mir gut.

I   like   that pullover.

The German sentence says, literally: 'The pullover *appeals to me*'. In German, the *thing* that you like is the *subject* (nominative), and the word(s) for the *person* is put in the *dative* case.

z.B.   **Gefällt dir der Rock**, Mutti?   Ja, **er gefällt mir** sehr gut.
      Do you like that skirt, Mum?   Yes, I like it very much.

In this last example, **er** is used for *it*, because we are referring back to **der Rock** (m.). This table shows the various possibilities in singular and plural:

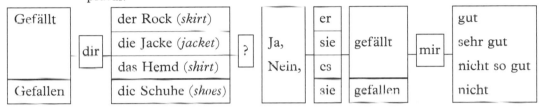

Gefällt		dir	der Rock (*skirt*)	?	Ja,	er	gefällt	mir	gut
			die Jacke (*jacket*)		Nein,	sie			sehr gut
			das Hemd (*shirt*)			es			nicht so gut
Gefallen			die Schuhe (*shoes*)			sie	gefallen		nicht

A dative noun as well as a pronoun can be used, as in the next example:

Dieses Buch gefällt **meinen Eltern** nicht.
My parents do not like this book.

NOTE that **gefallen** is a strong verb. The simple past is **gefiel** and the perfect is **hat gefallen**.

For more ways of expressing liking in German, see 12.4.

(c) schmecken

schmecken means *to taste*. It is used for discussing the flavour of food, and it behaves in very much the same way as **gefallen** (see (b) above). The food is the subject of the German sentence. The word(s) for the person who is enjoying (or not enjoying) the food is put in the dative.

z.B.   Wie **schmeckt dir der Schinken**?
      How do you like the ham?
      (literally: How does the ham taste to you?)

      Er schmeckt mir sehr gut, danke.
      It tastes very good (to me).

There need not be a person mentioned:

z.B.   **Dieser Kuchen schmeckt** ausgezeichnet.
      This cake tastes excellent.

      Diese Kartoffeln schmecken furchtbar.
      These potatoes taste awful.

When used on its own, **schmecken** implies 'to taste *good*'.

> z.B. Hat es geschmeckt?
> Did you enjoy it? (Did it taste good?)
>
> Das schmeckt!
> That tastes good!

(d) How to talk about how people are
The formula for this is: **es geht** + a person in the dative:

Wie geht's (= geht es) **dir**?	Es geht **mir** gut.
How are you?	I am fine.
Wie geht's **deinem Bruder**?	Es geht **mir** jetzt besser.
How's your brother?	I am better now.
Wie geht es **deinen Eltern**?	**Meiner Oma** geht es nicht so gut.
How are your parents?	My grandma is not very well.

(See also 12.2.)

> ! Do not say or write: „Ich bin gut", „Meine Oma ist besser", etc. These are wrong!

(e) Other health and 'state' expressions with the word(s) for the person in the dative
This table shows these and the way they work:

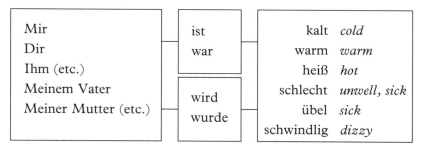

Mir	ist	kalt	*cold*
Dir	war	warm	*warm*
Ihm (etc.)		heiß	*hot*
Meinem Vater	wird	schlecht	*unwell, sick*
Meiner Mutter (etc.)	wurde	übel	*sick*
		schwindlig	*dizzy*

> z.B. **Mir** ist kalt.   **Ihr** wurde schwindlig.
> I'm cold.   She became/got dizzy.
>
> **Mir** wird kalt.   **Meinem Bruder** ist schlecht.
> I'm getting cold.   My brother feels funny/sick.
>
> **Ihm** war heiß   Ist **dir** warm?
> He was hot.   Are you warm?

> ! This is, more or less, a fixed list. These are the only adjectives that function in this way. Do not say or write, for instance, „Mir ist krank". This is not German!

10.31 ● Verbs with prepositions

Many verbs, both English and German, have one or more prepositions associated with them. English examples are:

to wait for   ⟶   I **waited for** the bus.

to think of   ⟶   I **thought of** you.

The verb and its preposition form a fixed phrase. German has many of these verbs followed by prepositions. Here is a useful selection:

warten auf + acc.   ⟶   Ich **wartete auf den Bus**.
to wait for   I waited for the bus.

denken an + acc.   ⟶   Ich **dachte an dich**.
to think of   I thought of you.

schreiben an + acc.   ⟶   Ich **schrieb an Maria**.
to write to   I wrote to Maria.

sich erinnern an + acc.   ⟶   Ich **erinnere mich an ihn**.
to remember   I remember him.

fragen nach + dat.   ⟶   Ich **fragte nach ihrem Mann**.
to ask about   I asked about her husband.

sich interessieren für + acc.   ⟶   Ich **interessiere mich für Sport**.
to be interested in   I'm interested in sport.

10.32 ● Infinitives: with and without *zu*

German clauses and sentences often have an infinitive at (or near) the end. This infinitive may or may not have **zu** before it.

(a) Infinitives without *zu*

There is no **zu** when the previous verb is:

a modal verb (see 10.8)

    z.B. Ich **will** nach Hause **fahren**.
           I want to go home.

werden (forming the future – see 10.29)

    z.B. Ich **werde** nach Hause **fahren**.
           I shall go home.

gehen   *to go and do something*

    z.B. Wir **gehen** morgen **einkaufen**.
           We're going shopping tomorrow.

sehen/hören   *to see or hear something happen*

    z.B. Ich **hörte** ihn ins Haus **kommen**.
           I heard him come into the house.

lassen   *to have something done for one* (see 10.7.c)

    z.B. Ich lasse mir die Haare **schneiden**.
           I'm having my hair cut.

Infinitives without **zu** are also used in commands and instructions (see 10.10.d).

Remember that in subordinate clauses (9.8), the infinitive is no longer the last word in the clause:

> z.B. Ich fahre in die Stadt, weil ich einen neuen Pullover **kaufen muß**.
> I'm going into town because I have to buy a new pullover.

(b) Infinitives with *zu*

Whenever infinitives are used in situations other than those listed in (a) above, **zu** is needed directly before the infinitive. There are many verbs and verbal phrases which are followed by **zu** and an infinitive. These are just a few examples:

versuchen   *to try*

> z.B. Ich **versuchte**, das Fenster **zu öffnen**.
> I tried to open the window.

beschließen   *to decide*

> z.B. Ich **habe beschlossen**, Physik **zu studieren**.
> I've decided to study physics.

Lust haben   *to feel like*

> z.B. Ich **habe keine Lust**, ins Kino **zu gehen**.
> I don't feel like going to the cinema.

sich darauf freuen   *to look forward to doing something*

> z.B. Ich **freue mich darauf**, dich **zu besuchen**.
> I'm looking forward to visiting you.

When **zu** is used with the infinitive of a separable verb, the **zu** is sandwiched into the middle:

> z.B. Ich habe vor, heute abend fern**zu**sehen.
> I'm intending to watch TV this evening.

Punctuation before *zu* + infinitive

All the above examples have a comma in the middle of the sentence. This is needed as long as the **zu** + infinitive clause has some other word or words connected with it. In the first example above, these other words were **das Fenster**. However, when **zu** + infinitive is used without any accompanying word or phrase, no comma is inserted:

> z.B. Ich habe keine Lust **zu singen**.
> I don't feel like singing.

One clause at a time

It sounds more natural to complete the verb already begun before starting a **zu** + infinitive clause:

> z.B. Es **fing an** zu regnen.   Das Baby **hörte auf** zu weinen.
> It **started** to rain.   The baby **stopped** crying.

(BUT it is not wrong to leave the **an** and **auf** to the end of the sentence.)

statt zu + **infinitive and** *ohne zu* + **infinitive**
statt zu + infinitive (sometimes **anstatt zu** + infinitive) means *instead of doing something*:

> z.B. **Statt zu halten**, fuhr Karsten weiter.
> Instead of stopping, Karsten drove on.

ohne zu + infinitive means *without doing something*:

An der Ampel fuhr er bei Rot durch, **ohne** den Polizisten **zu sehen**.
At the traffic-lights he went through on red, without seeing the policeman.

There must be a comma separating the **statt zu** or **ohne zu** clause from the rest of the sentence.

⊶ 10.33 ● *um zu* + **infinitive**

This is the German way of saying *in order to do something*, as in this table of examples:

Ich bleibe zu Hause, *I'm staying at home* [compulsory comma]	**um zu** arbeiten	*in order to work*
	um Schach **zu** spielen	*in order to play chess*
	um fern**zu**sehen	*in order to watch TV*
	um einen Brief **zu** schreiben	*in order to write a letter*

NOTE that in the third example, as always, **zu** is sandwiched into the middle of a separable verb.

In the second and fourth examples, notice that there can be a direct object (**Schach** and **einen Brief**) sandwiched between **um** and the **zu** + infinitive.

! In English, we often leave out the words *in order* and say simply:

> e.g. I'm staying at home *to work*.

However, when the underlying meaning is *in order to*, you must use **um zu** + infinitive in German.

10.34 ● The passive – *das Passiv*

Active and passive – what are they?
Most sentences are *active*: a subject 'acts', i.e. does an action.

> e.g. A policeman arrested the burglar.

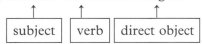

subject	verb	direct object

Some sentences, including this one, can also be expressed less directly, in the *passive*, like this:

> The burglar was arrested by a policeman.

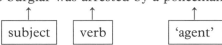

subject	verb	'agent'

NOTE that the *direct object* of the original active sentence has become the *subject* of the passive sentence:

Active: A policeman arrested **the burglar**.

Passive: **The burglar** was arrested by a policeman.

The subject of the active sentence becomes the 'agent' in a passive sentence. In English, the agent has *by* in front of it: *by a policeman*. The agent is often simply left out, however:

The burglar was arrested.

If we translate this example sentence into German, we shall see how to construct passive sentences:

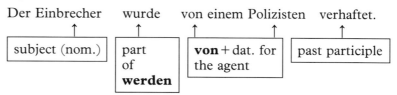

Der Einbrecher   wurde   von einem Polizisten   verhaftet.

| subject (nom.) | part of **werden** | **von** + dat. for the agent | past participle |

This example shows that the passive is formed from these two elements: the relevant tense of **werden** (this is a past tense sentence, so the simple past **wurde** is used) *plus* a past participle (see 10.17) at the end of the clause or sentence.

Examples of the passive with other tenses and verb forms (NOTE the changes in word order):

Present: Diese Kirche **wird** von vielen Touristen **fotografiert**.
          This church **is photographed** by many tourists.

Modal: Diese Milch **muß** sofort **getrunken werden**.
        This milk **must be drunk** immediately.

Perfect: Meine Autoschlüssel **sind gestohlen worden**.
        My car-keys **have been stolen**

The last example is the most complex. It consists of the perfect tense of **werden**, which is shortened from **sind geworden** to **sind worden** in the passive, *plus* the past participle, **gestohlen**.

10.35 ● The subjunctive – *der Konjunktiv*

What is the subjunctive?

The subjunctive is a set of verb forms which are needed in certain types of sentence in German. When the subjunctive is used, it lends a touch of uncertainty or wishful thinking to a sentence. However, you do not use the subjunctive whenever you feel like it. It is used in certain situations only, and these are explained in later sections (10.38 Reported speech, 10.39 Conditional sentences, 10.40 Other uses of the subjunctive).

The subjunctive has two main 'tenses'. (I put the word in inverted commas because, unlike ordinary tenses, the 'tenses' of the subjunctive are not connected with different times.) These two tenses are *subjunctive I* and *subjunctive II*. These are sometimes known, rather confusingly, as the present and past subjunctive.

10.36 ● **Subjunctive I**

To make subjunctive I, take the stem of the verb and add the subjunctive endings. As an example, here is the verb **fahren** (*to go*):

ich fahr**e**	wir fahr**en**
du fahr**est**	ihr fahr**et**
er/sie/es fahr**e** [no **t** ending]	Sie/sie fahr**en**

NOTE that all the subjunctive endings contain **e**. The **ich** and **er/sie/es** parts are always identical in the subjunctive.

fahren is a strong verb which modifies its stem in the ordinary present tense (see 10.5). There is no stem modification in the subjunctive.

Only one verb has an irregular subjunctive I. This verb is **sein** (*to be*):

ich **sei**	wir **seien**
du **seist/seiest**	ihr **seiet**
er/sie/es **sei**	Sie/sie **seien**

10.37 ● **Subjunctive II**

For weak verbs, subjunctive II is identical to the ordinary simple past –

z.B. ich spielte, ich wohnte, ich arbeitete.

For strong verbs, take the ordinary simple past form, add the subjunctive endings (the same ones as for subjunctive I) and, if possible, add Umlaut:

z.B. gehen *to go*

ich ging**e**	wir ging**en**
du ging**est**	ihr ging**et**
er/sie/es ging**e**	Sie/sie ging**en**

This is formed from the simple past of **gehen**, which is **ging**. Umlaut could not be added to **ging**, because it can be added only to **a**, **o** or **u**. Other subjunctive II forms are: **wäre** (from **sein**), **führe** (from **fahren**), **käme** (from **kommen**), etc.

Here are the subjunctive II forms of modal verbs:

können ⟶	ich **könnte**	sollen ⟶	ich **sollte**
müssen ⟶	ich **müßte**	dürfen ⟶	ich **dürfte**
wollen ⟶	ich **wollte**	mögen ⟶	ich **möchte**

Compare these with their ordinary simple past forms in 10.15.

! NOTE that **wollte** and **sollte** never have Umlaut.

Common irregular verbs:

haben ⟶	ich **hätte**	werden ⟶	ich **würde**
wissen ⟶	ich **wüßte**	bringen ⟶	ich **brächte**

Compare these with their ordinary simple past forms in 10.16.

10.38 ● Reported speech (indirekte Rede)

(a) What is reported speech?

Reported speech, as the name suggests, is the reporting of someone's words:

> e.g. He said that he had no money.
> She said her father was ill.
> He asked whether we could help him.

The above are reported versions of these original words:

> 'I have no money.'
> 'My father is ill.'
> 'Can you help me?'

In German, the subjunctive is the most common way of showing that someone's words are being reported. If we translate the first English example above into German, we get:

> Er sagte, daß er kein Geld **habe**.

habe is a subjunctive I form. Do *not* use the simple past (**hatte**) here.

(b) Subjunctive I or subjunctive II in reported speech?

You can use either! The important thing is to use a *distinctively subjunctive* form – i.e. *not* one which is identical with either the ordinary present or simple past tenses. These examples will make the point clear:

Peter sagte, daß er krank **sei/wäre**. Peter said that he **was** ill.	[both are distinctively subjunctive, so both are possible]
Peter sagte, daß er in London **wohne**. Peter said that he **lived** in London.	**wohnte** would be identical with the simple past, so it cannot be used

In written German, there is a preference for subjunctive I in reported speech, when this provides a distinctive form.

Study these further examples to see how to construct various types of reported speech:

> Petra sagte, daß sie nicht **mitkommen könne/könnte**.
> Petra said that she **could not come** with us.
>
> Peter sagte, daß er den Film nicht **gesehen habe/hätte**.
> Peter said that **he had** not **seen** the film.
>
> Petra sagte, daß sie mit dem Taxi **gefahren sei/wäre**.
> Petra said that she **had gone** by taxi.
>
> Peter sagte, daß er ein Auto **kaufen werde/würde**.
> Peter said that he **was going to buy** a car.

The last of the above examples shows what to do when the original words referred to the future. (Here they must have been: *I am going to buy a car'*.) In German, **werde** or **würde** (*would*) is used with an infinitive.

Leaving out daß

In all of the above examples, **daß** could have been left out. When this happens, there is still a comma, but the verb is not sent to the end:

> z.B. Peter sagte**,** er **sei/wäre** krank.
> Peter said he **was** ill.

(c) Reported questions

In reported questions, **ob** is used for *whether* or *if* (*not* **wenn**!), but the ordinary question words are often needed (see section 5):

z.B.   Petra fragte, **ob** ich Geschwister **hätte**.
           [not **habe**, which is not distinctive]
        Petra asked **whether/if** I **had** any brothers or sisters.

        Peter fragte mich, **ob** ich zur Party **gehen möchte**.
           [**möchte** = would like to]
        Peter asked me **whether** I **would like to go** to the party.

        Petra fragte, **ob** wir ihr **helfen könnten**
           [**können** would not be distinctive]
        Petra asked **whether** we **could help** her.

        Peter fragte, **wann** der Zug **ankommen würde**.
        Peter asked **when** the train **would/was going to arrive**.

        Petra fragte, **wo** die Polizeiwache **sei/wäre**.
        Petra asked **where** the police station **was**.

(d) Reported commands

She asked me to open the door, etc.

When the verb is *ask*, German uses the verb **bitten** with a similar sentence construction to the English one:

z.B.   Sie **bat** mich, die Tür **aufzumachen**.
        She **asked** me **to open** the door.

She told me to open the door, etc.

With other verbs (such as *tell*), a different construction is needed in German:

        Sie **sagte mir**, **daß** ich die Tür **aufmachen sollte**.   [OR: **müßte**]

Leaving out *daß*:

        Sie **sagte mir**, ich **sollte** [OR: **müßte**] die Tür **aufmachen**.
        She **told me to open** the door.

The German sentence literally says: *She said to me that I should* [OR: *had to*] *open the door*.

(e) Reported speech without the subjunctive

When the verb of saying (e.g. **sagen**, **fragen**) is in a tense other than the past, ordinary tenses are often used instead of the subjunctive. In spoken German, the subjunctive is often avoided even after **sagte** and **fragte**. However, the tenses used are not the past tenses that we use in English:

z.B.   Peter hat mir gesagt, daß er krank **ist**.
        Peter told me that he **was** ill.

German uses the same tense as the original words (e.g. 'I *am* ill' – present tense).

10.39 ● Conditional sentences

What are conditional sentences?

These are sentences which involve *if* in English. There are two types. So-called 'real' conditional sentences are about things which are perfectly likely to happen:

> e.g. If I **have** enough money, I'**ll buy** a house.

This is straightforward in German:

> **Wenn** ich genug Geld **habe**, **kaufe** ich ein Haus.

The verbs are in the ordinary present tense.

'Unreal' conditional sentences are about things which are very unlikely to happen. Often, they describe wishful thinking:

> e.g. If I **had** enough money, I **would buy** a house.

The point here is that the speaker has *not* got enough money and in fact can*not* buy a house. He is just imagining what *might be*.

In German, unreal conditional sentences require *subjunctive II in both clauses*. Subjunctive I *cannot* be used! In theory, any subjunctive II forms can be used, but in practice only the most frequently used verbs are normally put into subjunctive II. These verbs are **sein** (*to be*), **haben** (*to have*) and the modal verbs (see 10.8). For other verbs, their subjunctive II form is replaced by **würde** + infinitive. Study these examples:

> Wenn ich reich **wäre**, **würde ich** einen Porsche kaufen.
> If I **were** rich I **would buy** a Porsche.
>
> Wenn ich eine Million Mark **gewinnen würde**, **wäre** ich sehr glücklich.
> If I **won** a million Marks, I **would be** very happy.
>
> Wenn ich viel Geld **hätte**, **könnte** ich eine Weltreise **machen**.
> If I **had** a lot of money I **could** [OR: **would be able to**] **go** on a world tour.
>
> Ich **wäre** sehr dankbar, wenn Sie mir **helfen könnten**.
> I **would be** very grateful if you **could help** me.

Remember: Verb forms based on subjunctive II are used in *both* clauses.

> ❗

konnte or *könnte*?

Both of these mean *could*, but they are not the same!

konnte is the simple past tense and means *was able to*:

> z.B. Gestern **konnte** ich **nicht** schwimmen gehen.
> Yesterday I **couldn't** (= **was not able to**) go swimming.

könnte is subjunctive II and means *would be able to* or *might be able to*:

> z.B. Wenn das Wetter schön **wäre**, **könnte** ich schwimmen gehen.
> If the weather were nice, I **could** (= **would be able to**) go swimming.
>
> **Könnten Sie** mir bitte helfen?
> **Could you** (= **Might you be able to**) help me?

10.40 ● **Other uses of the subjunctive**

Here are some other uses of the subjunctive that you are likely to meet:

(a) Subjunctive II as a polite form

hätte, **wäre** and **könnte** are often used as polite forms. They seem less abrupt than the ordinary present tenses of **haben**, **sein** or **können** in examples like these:

> Das **wäre** alles. (= Das **ist** alles)
> That's all.
>
> **Hättest** (= **Hast**) du Lust mitzukommen?
> Do you feel like coming with us?
>
> **Könntest** (= **Kannst**) du mir helfen?
> Could/Can you help me?

(b) *als ob* ('as if')

als ob is often followed by ordinary tenses, but in past tense sentences it usually requires the subjunctive:

> z.B.   Er sah aus, **als ob** er krank **sei/wäre**.
> He looked **as if** he **was/were** ill.

(c) How to express 'could have' and 'should have'

These two examples show how:

> Du **hättest** gestern **mitkommen können**.
> You **could have come** with us yesterday.
>
> Du **hättest** gestern **mitkommen sollen**.
> You **should have come** with us yesterday.

10.41 ● **Other points about verbs**

(a) How to express 'there is' and 'there are'

For *there is* and *there are*, German usually uses **es gibt** + accusative:

Es gibt viel Verkehr heute.   Was **gibt** es heute im Fernsehen?
There's a lot of traffic today.   What **is there** on TV today?

Es gibt Fisch zum Abendessen.
There's fish for supper.

To indicate that something is in a specific place, **es ist/sind** + nominative is used:

Es ist ein Mann an der Tür.
There's a man at the door.

Es sind zwei Hefte auf dem Tisch.
There are two exercise books on the table.

(b) To want somebody to do something

wollen (see 10.8) is used when the subject of the sentence wants to do something:

> z.B.   **Ich will** das Mittagessen **kochen**.
> **I want to cook** the lunch.

When the subject wants *somebody else* to do something, the following construction is required:

> **Ich will**, daß **Martin** das Mittagessen **kocht**.
> **I want Martin to cook** the lunch (literally: 'I want that Martin cooks the lunch').

10.42 ● English verbs with more than one German equivalent

Here, in alphabetical order, are some of the common English verbs that cause problems for learners of German because they have more than one German equivalent. (Verbs marked ★ take **sein** in the perfect tense – see 10.22)

! **answer**		
to answer a person:	**antworten** + dat.	Er **antwortete ihr** nicht. He did not answer her.
to answer a thing:	**antworten auf** + acc.	Er **antwortete auf meinen Brief**.
	or: **beantworten** + acc.	Er **beantwortete meinen Brief**. He answered my letter.

! **ask**		
to ask a question:	**fragen** + acc.	Ich **fragte ihn**, wo er wohne. I asked him where he lived.
to ask after/about:	**fragen nach** + dat.	Ich **fragte nach ihrer Mutter**. I asked about her mother.
to ask for something:	**bitten** + acc. **um** + acc.	Ich **bat ihn um eine** Briefmarke. I asked him for a stamp.
to ask someone to do something:	**bitten** + acc. **zu** + inf.	Ich **bat sie, mich zu besuchen**. I asked her to visit me.

! **go**		
to go on foot:	**gehen**★	Wir **gingen** durch den Wald. We went through the forest.
to go in a vehicle:	**fahren**★	Wir **fuhren** nach Frankreich. We went to France.

! **know**		
to know information:	**wissen**	Die Antwort **weiß** ich nicht. I do not know the answer.
to be acquainted with:	**kennen**	Ich **kenne** ihn nicht. I do not know him.

! **leave**

to leave something somewhere:	**lassen/*zurück*lassen**	Ich **ließ** mein Buch zu Hause (**zurück**). I left my book (behind) at home.
to leave someone *or* somewhere:	**verlassen** + acc. (*must* have a direct object)	Ich **verließ das Haus** um acht. I left the house at eight.
to depart/set off:	***ab*fahren★/*los*fahren★** (no direct object)	Der Zug **fuhr** um acht Uhr **ab**. The train left at eight o'clock.
		Wir **fuhren** gleich **los**. We set off straightaway.

! **like**

see 12.4, and for **gefallen** see also 10.30.b.

! **live**

to live one's life:	**leben**	Bismarck **lebte** im 19. Jahrhundert. Bismarck lived in the 19th century.
to inhabit somewhere:	**wohnen**	Wir **wohnen** in einem Dorf. We live in a village.

! **look**

to have an appearance:	***aus*sehen**	Du **siehst** schick **aus**. You look smart.
to look with one's eyes:	**sehen/schauen** (also, in conversation: **gucken**)	**Sieh/Schau** mal! **Guck** mal! Just look!
to look at someone/something:	***an*sehen**	Der Polizist **sah** mich **an**. The policeman looked at me.
to look at something:	**sehen auf** + acc.	Er **sah auf** seine Uhr. He looked at his watch.

! **meet**

most meanings of *meet*:	**treffen** + acc. (*must* have a direct object)	Jan **traf** Ute vor dem Kino. Jan met Ute outside the cinema.
to meet one another:	**sich treffen**	Wo **treffen** wir **uns**? Where shall we meet (one another)?
to meet by chance:	**begegnen★** + dat.	Udo **ist mir** gestern **begegnet**. Udo met me (by chance) yesterday.

to collect/call for someone:	*ab***holen**	Jutta **holte** mich am Bahnhof **ab**. Jutta met me at the station.
to make someone's acquaintance:	*kennen***lernen**	Ich freue mich darauf, deine Eltern **kennenzulernen**. I'm looking forward to meeting your parents.

!	**prefer**

see 12.4

!	**put**		
	to lay something down:	**legen** (regular!)	Ich **legte** das Buch auf den Tisch. I put the book on the table.
	to stand something up:	**stellen**	Ich **stellte** das Glas auf den Tisch. I put the glass on the table.
	to insert:	**stecken**	Ich **steckte** den Brief in den Umschlag. I put the letter in the envelope.
	general meanings of *put*:	**tun**	Ich **tat** Fett in die Pfanne. I put some fat in the frying-pan.

Do not confuse **legen** and **liegen**.
Legen means *put* as shown above.
Liegen means *lie* and shows a position: Das Buch **liegt** auf dem Tisch.
         The book is lying on the table.

!	**sit**		
	to sit down (motion):	sich *hin***setzen/** sich **setzen** (regular)	Ich **setzte mich** auf das Sofa (**hin**). I sat down on the sofa.
	to sit (position):	**sitzen** (strong)	Ich **saß** immer auf dem Sofa. I always sat on the sofa.

!	**spend**		
	to spend money:	*aus***geben**	Gestern **gab** ich hundert Mark **aus**. Yesterday I spent a hundred Marks.
	to spend time:	**verbringen**	Ich **verbrachte** die Ferien in Rom. I spent the holidays in Rome.

!	stay		
	to remain:	**bleiben***	Ich **blieb** zwei Tage in Berlin. I stayed in Berlin for two days.
	to live somewhere for a while	**wohnen**	Ich **wohnte** in einem Hotel. I stayed in a hotel.
	to stay overnight:	**übernachten**	Ich **übernachtete** in einem Hotel. I stayed overnight in a hotel.

!	stop		
	to stop travelling:	**halten**	Warum **hat** der Zug hier **gehalten**? Why has the train stopped here?
	to stop walking:	*stehen*bleiben*	Er **blieb** vor unserem Haus **stehen**. He stopped outside our house.
	to make someone else stop:	*an*halten	Ein Polizist **hielt** uns **an**. A policeman stopped us.
	to cease an activity:	*auf*hören zu + inf.	Wir **hörten auf zu arbeiten**. We stopped working.

!	take		
	basic meanings of take:	**nehmen**	Ich **nahm** das Buch von dem Tisch. I took the book from the table. Ich **nahm** den Bus. I took the bus.
	to transport/accompany:	**bringen**	Er **brachte** mich nach Hause. He took me home.
	to take time:	**brauchen**	Ich **brauche** zwei Stunden, um meine Hausaufgaben zu machen. It takes me two hours to do my homework. (literally: 'I need . . .')

!	wake up		
	to stop sleeping:	*auf*wachen*	Ich **bin** um acht Uhr **aufgewacht**. I woke up at eight o'clock.
	to wake someone else up:	**wecken**	Ich **weckte** meinen Bruder um neun. I woke my brother up at nine.

• **Verb list**

This is a list of all the strong and irregular verbs you are likely to meet. The most essential verbs for speaking and writing your own German are marked with a spot (•). Many of the most common separable and inseparable verbs have been included on the list, but there was not room for them all. To find out how these verbs work, look up the basic verb. For example, to find out how *auf*schlagen works, look up **schlagen**. From the four forms given here, all the other verb forms can be worked out.

Infinitive	Present tense (er/sie/es form)	Simple past tense (er/sie/es form)	Perfect tense (er/sie/es form)	English meaning
abbiegen	biegt. . .ab	bog. . .ab	ist abgebogen	*to turn off (a road)*
• **ab**fahren	fährt. . .ab	fuhr. . .ab	ist abgefahren	*to depart*
• **ab**waschen	wäscht. . .ab	wusch. . .ab	hat abgewaschen	*to wash up*
anbieten	bietet. . .an	bot. . .an	hat angeboten	*to offer*
• **an**fangen	fängt. . .an	fing. . .an	hat angefangen	*to start*
• **an**kommen	kommt. . .an	kam. . .an	ist angekommen	*to arrive*
• **an**rufen	ruft. . .an	rief. . .an	hat angerufen	*to ring someone up*
anstreichen	streicht. . .an	strich. . .an	hat angestrichen	*to paint (houses, etc.)*
• **an**ziehen	zieht. . .an	zog. . .an	hat angezogen	*to put on (clothes)*
aufheben	hebt. . .auf	hob. . .auf	hat aufgehoben	*to pick something up; to keep*
• **auf**stehen	steht. . .auf	stand. . .auf	ist aufgestanden	*to get up*
• **aus**geben	gibt. . .aus	gab. . .aus	hat ausgegeben	*to spend (money)*
• **aus**sehen	sieht. . .aus	sah. . .aus	hat ausgesehen	*to look, appear*
• **aus**steigen	steigt. . .aus	stieg. . .aus	ist ausgestiegen	*to get off/out*
• **aus**ziehen	zieht. . .aus	zog. . .aus	hat ausgezogen	*to take off (clothes)*
backen	bäckt/backt	backte	hat gebacken	*to bake*
befehlen	befiehlt	befahl	hat befohlen	*to order someone to . . .*
• beginnen	beginnt	begann	hat begonnen	*to begin*
behalten	behält	behielt	hat behalten	*to keep*
beißen	beißt	biß	hat gebissen	*to bite*

A

B

• bekommen	bekommt	bekam	hat bekommen	*to get, receive*
• beschließen	beschließt	beschloß	hat beschlossen	*to decide*
• beschreiben	beschreibt	beschrieb	hat beschrieben	*to describe*
besitzen	besitzt	besaß	hat besessen	*to own*
biegen	biegt	bog	hat gebogen	*to bend*
bieten	bietet	bot	hat geboten	*to offer*
binden	bindet	band	hat gebunden	*to tie*
• bitten	bittet	bat	hat gebeten	*to ask*
blasen	bläst	blies	hat geblasen	*to blow*
• bleiben	bleibt	blieb	ist geblieben	*to stay, remain*
braten	brät	briet	hat gebraten	*to fry; to roast*
• brechen	bricht	brach	hat gebrochen	*to break; to vomit*
brennen	brennt	brannte	hat gebrannt	*to burn, be on fire*
• bringen	bringt	brachte	hat gebracht	*to bring, take*

D	denken	denkt	dachte	hat gedacht	*to think*
	• dürfen	darf	durfte	hat (inf.) dürfen	*to be allowed to (see 10.8)*

E	• **ein**laden	lädt. . .ein	lud. . .ein	hat eingeladen	*to invite*
	• **ein**schlafen	schläft. . .ein	schlief. . .ein	ist eingeschlafen	*to go to sleep*
	• **ein**steigen	steigt. . .ein	stieg. . .ein	ist eingestiegen	*to get in/on*
	empfangen	empfängt	empfing	hat empfangen	*to receive*
	empfehlen	empfiehlt	empfahl	hat empfohlen	*to recommend*
	sich entscheiden	entscheidet sich	entschied sich	hat sich entschieden	*to decide*
	sich entschließen	entschließt sich	entschloß sich	hat sich entschlossen	*to make up one's mind*
	erhalten	erhält	erhielt	hat erhalten	*to receive*
	erkennen	erkennt	erkannte	hat erkannt	*to recognise*
	erscheinen	erscheint	erschien	ist erschienen	*to appear*
	erschrecken	erschrickt	erschrak	ist erschrocken	*to get a fright*
	• essen	ißt	aß	hat gegessen	*to eat*

F	• fahren	fährt	fuhr	ist gefahren	*to go; to drive (see 10.22.e)*
	• fallen	fällt	fiel	ist gefallen	*to fall*
	fangen	fängt	fing	hat gefangen	*to catch*
	• **fern**sehen	sieht. . .fern	sah. . .fern	hat ferngesehen	*to watch* TV
	• finden	findet	fand	hat gefunden	*to find*
	• fliegen	fliegt	flog	ist geflogen	*to fly*

Infinitive	Present tense (er/sie/es form)	Simple past tense (er/sie/es form)	Perfect tense (er/sie/es form)	English meaning
fliehen	flieht	floh	ist geflohen	*to flee, escape*
fließen	fließt	floß	ist geflossen	*to flow*
fressen	frißt	fraß	hat gefressen	*to eat (used when animals eat)*
frieren	friert	fror	hat gefroren	*to freeze, be cold*
G • geben	gibt	gab	hat gegeben	*to give*
• gefallen	gefällt	gefiel	hat gefallen	*to appeal to*
• gehen	geht	ging	ist gegangen	*to go, walk*
gelingen	gelingt	gelang	ist gelungen	*to succeed*
genießen	genießt	genoß	hat genossen	*to enjoy*
• geschehen	geschieht	geschah	ist geschehen	*to happen*
• gewinnen	gewinnt	gewann	hat gewonnen	*to win*
gießen	gießt	goß	hat gegossen	*to pour; to water; to pour down*
gleiten	gleitet	glitt	ist geglitten	*to slide, glide*
graben	gräbt	grub	hat gegraben	*to dig*
greifen	greift	griff	hat gegriffen	*to grab, seize*
H • haben	hat	hatte	hat gehabt	*to have (see 10.9)*
• halten	hält	hielt	hat gehalten	*to hold; to stop*
hängen	hängt	hing	hat gehangen	*to hang*
heben	hebt	hob	hat gehoben	*to raise, lift*
• heißen	heißt	hieß	hat geheißen	*to mean; to be called*
• helfen	hilft	half	hat geholfen	*to help*
K • kennen	kennt	kannte	hat gekannt	*to know*
klingen	klingt	klang	hat geklungen	*to sound (odd, etc.)*
• kommen	kommt	kam	ist gekommen	*to come*
• können	kann	konnte	hat (inf.) können	*to be able to, can (see 10.8)*
kriechen	kriecht	kroch	ist gekrochen	*to crawl; to creep*
L • lassen	läßt	ließ	hat gelassen	*to leave something somewhere*
• laufen	läuft	lief	ist gelaufen	*to run, walk*
leiden	leidet	litt	hat gelitten	*to suffer*

106

leihen	leiht	lieh	hat geliehen	*to lend; to borrow*
• lesen	liest	las	hat gelesen	*to read*
• liegen	liegt	lag	hat gelegen	*to lie (position)*
lügen	lügt	log	hat gelogen	*to lie (tell lies)*

M messen	mißt	maß	hat gemessen	*to measure*
• mögen	mag	mochte	hat gemocht	*to like* (see 10.8)
• müssen	muß	mußte	hat (inf.) müssen	*to have to, must* (see 10.8)

N • nehmen	nimmt	nahm	hat genommen	*to take*
nennen	nennt	nannte	hat genannt	*to name, call*

P pfeifen	pfeift	pfiff	hat gepfiffen	*to whistle*

R • **rad**fahren	fährt. . .**R**ad	fuhr. . .**R**ad	ist radgefahren	*to cycle*
raten	rät	riet	hat geraten	*to advise; to guess*
reißen	reißt	riß	hat gerissen	*to tear, rip*
reiten	reitet	ritt	ist geritten	*to ride (horses)*
• rennen	rennt	rannte	ist gerannt	*to run*
riechen	riecht	roch	hat gerochen	*to smell*
• rufen	ruft	rief	hat gerufen	*to shout, call*

S • scheinen	scheint	schien	hat geschienen	*to shine; to seem*
schieben	schiebt	schob	hat geschoben	*to push*
schießen	schießt	schoß	hat geschossen	*to shoot*
• schlafen	schläft	schlief	hat geschlafen	*to sleep*
schlagen	schlägt	schlug	hat geschlagen	*to hit, beat, strike*
• schließen	schließt	schloß	hat geschlossen	*to close*
schmeißen	schmeißt	schmiß	hat geschmissen	*to chuck, throw (informal)*
schneiden	schneidet	schnitt	hat geschnitten	*to cut*
• schreiben	schreibt	schrieb	hat geschrieben	*to write*
schreien	schreit	schrie	hat geschrien	*to scream, shout*
schweigen	schweigt	schwieg	hat geschwiegen	*to be silent*
• schwimmen	schwimmt	schwamm	ist geschwommen	*to swim*
• sehen	sieht	sah	hat gesehen	*to see*
• sein	ist	war	ist gewesen	*to be* (see 10.9)
• singen	singt	sang	hat gesungen	*to sing*
sinken	sinkt	sank	ist gesunken	*to sink*

Infinitive	Present tense (er/sie/es form)	Simple past tense (er/sie/es form)	Perfect tense (er/sie/es form)	English meaning
• sitzen	sitzt	saß	hat gesessen	*to sit*
skilaufen	läuft. . .**Ski**	lief. . .**Ski**	ist skigelaufen	*to ski*
• sollen	soll	sollte	hat (inf.) sollen	*to be supposed to (see 10.8)*
• sprechen	spricht	sprach	hat gesprochen	*to speak*
springen	springt	sprang	ist gesprungen	*to jump*
• stehen	steht	stand	hat gestanden	*to stand*
• stehlen	stiehlt	stahl	hat gestohlen	*to steal*
steigen	steigt	stieg	ist gestiegen	*to climb, go up*
• sterben	stirbt	starb	ist gestorben	*to die*
stinken	stinkt	stank	hat gestunken	*to stink*
stoßen	stößt	stieß	hat gestoßen	*to push, shove, poke*
streichen	streicht	strich	hat gestrichen	*to stroke; to paint; to cross out*
sich streiten	streitet sich	stritt sich	hat sich gestritten	*to quarrel*
T • tragen	trägt	trug	hat getragen	*to carry; to wear*
• treffen	trifft	traf	hat getroffen	*to meet someone*
treiben	treibt	trieb	hat getrieben	*to drive; to do (an activity)*
treten	tritt	trat	**ist** getreten	*to step*
treten	tritt	trat	**hat** getreten	*to kick*
• trinken	trinkt	trank	hat getrunken	*to drink*
• tun	tut	tat	hat getan	*to do; to put*
U überfahren	überfährt	überfuhr	hat überfahren	*to run over someone*
übertreiben	übertreibt	übertrieb	hat übertrieben	*to exaggerate*
umziehen	zieht. . .**um**	zog. . .**um**	ist umgezogen	*to move house*
• sich **um**ziehen	zieht sich . . . **um**	zog sich. . .**um**	hat sich umgezogen	*to get changed*
unterbrechen	unterbricht	unterbrach	hat unterbrochen	*to interrupt*
unterhalten	unterhält	unterhielt	hat unterhalten	*to entertain*
unterschreiben	unterschreibt	unterschrieb	hat unterschrieben	*to sign*

V				
verbergen	verbirgt	verbarg	hat verborgen	*to hide*
verbieten	verbietet	verbot	hat verboten	*to forbid*
• verbringen	verbringt	verbrachte	hat verbracht	*to spend (time)*
• vergessen	vergißt	vergaß	hat vergessen	*to forget*
vergleichen	vergleicht	verglich	hat verglichen	*to compare*
• verlassen	verläßt	verließ	hat verlassen	*to leave someone/ somewhere*
• verlieren	verliert	verlor	hat verloren	*to lose*
vermeiden	vermeidet	vermied	hat vermieden	*to avoid*
verschlafen	verschläft	verschlief	hat verschlafen	*to oversleep*
verschreiben	verschreibt	verschrieb	hat verschrieben	*to prescribe*
verschwinden	verschwindet	verschwand	ist verschwunden	*to disappear*
versprechen	verspricht	versprach	hat versprochen	*to promise*
• verstehen	versteht	verstand	hat verstanden	*to understand*
verzeihen	verzeiht	verzieh	hat verziehen	*to pardon, excuse*
vorschlagen	schlägt. . .vor	schlug. . .vor	hat vorgeschlagen	*to suggest*

W				
wachsen	wächst	wuchs	ist gewachsen	*to grow*
• waschen	wäscht	wusch	hat gewaschen	*to wash*
• werden	wird	wurde	ist geworden	*to become (see 10.9)*
werfen	wirft	warf	hat geworfen	*to throw*
• wiegen	wiegt	wog	hat gewogen	*to weigh*
• wissen	weiß	wußte	hat gewußt	*to know (see 10.9)*
• wollen	will	wollte	hat (inf.) wollen	*to want to (see 10.8)*

Z				
zerbrechen	zerbricht	zerbrach	hat zerbrochen	*to break, smash*
ziehen	zieht	zog	hat gezogen	*to pull*
zugreifen	greift. . .zu	griff. . .zu	hat zugegriffen	*to help oneself*
zusammenstoßen	stößt. . .zusammen	stieß. . .zusammen	ist zusammengestoßen	*to collide, crash*
zwingen	zwingt	zwang	hat gezwungen	*to force, compel*

alphabet
spelling
punctuation

11

11.1 ● The alphabet

The German alphabet is the same as the English one. Here are the names of the letters to use when spelling aloud. There is no official spelling for the names of the letters, but those given here will give the correct names if they are pronounced like German words.

A	Ah	G	Geh	M	Emm	S	Eß	Y	Ypsilon
B	Beh	H	Hah	N	Enn	T	Teh	Z	Zett
C	Zeh	I	Ih	O	Oh	U	Uh		
D	Deh	J	Jot	P	Peh	V	Fau		
E	Eh	K	Kah	Q	Kuh	W	Weh		
F	Eff	L	Ell	R	Err	X	Icks		

The double *s* symbol (**ß**) is called **Eszett**, and vowels with Umlaut are called:

Ä Äh   Ö Öh   Ü Üh

To say, for example, *double P* in German, say **zwei P**.

11.2 ● Capital letters

! Do not forget that all German nouns must be given a capital letter. However, adjectives do not have capitals:

z.B. Wir haben einen **d**eutschen **W**agen.
We have a **G**erman **c**ar.

11.3 ● ß (Eszett)

These are the rules for when to write **ß** and when to write **ss**:

Rule 1: Always write **ß**, *except between two short vowels.*

> z.B.   Fluß (*river*), vergißt (*forgets*), Füße (*feet*)

The **ü** is long in Füße. Contrast these examples with:

> z.B.   Flüsse (*rivers*), verpassen (*to miss*), messen (*to measure*)

In these examples, there are short vowels on either side of the **ss**.

Rule 2: In capital letters, **ß** does not exist, so we must write **SS**.

NOTE that some nouns and verbs alternate between **ß** and **ss**, because of Rule 1 above.

> z.B.   der Paß (*passport*) changes in the plural to Pässe.
> verpassen (*to miss*) changes in the **er/sie/es** form of the present tense to verpaßt, and its simple past form is verpaßte.

11.4 ● German punctuation

. Punkt	! Ausrufezeichen/Ausrufungszeichen
, Komma	? Fragezeichen
: Doppelpunkt	– Gedankenstrich
; Strichpunkt/Semikolon	„" Anführungszeichen/Anführungsstriche

In dictations, you will also hear:

> Anführungszeichen unten   *open inverted commas*
> Anführungszeichen oben   *close inverted commas*

NOTE how direct speech is punctuated:

> Hans fragte: „Wie heißt du?"
> „Wie heißt du?", fragte Hans.
> Petra sagte: „Ich komme aus Berlin."
> „Ich komme aus Berlin", sagte Petra.
> „Ich komme", sagte Petra, „aus Berlin."

11.5 ● When to use commas

The rules can be found in the following sections: 9.7.b, 9.8, 9.9, 10.32.b and 10.33.

11.6 ● Abbreviations

There are hundreds of abbreviations used in German, as there are in English, but here are just a few that you will frequently come across.

> bzw. = beziehungsweise *or as the case may be*
> d.h. = das heißt *that is/i.e.*
> usw. = und so weiter *and so on/etc.*
> z.B. = zum Beispiel *for example/e.g.*

how to say it

Notes

1 For *you,* **du** is mostly used here. Often, of course, you will need to use the **Sie** form. (For **du** and **Sie** see 4.3.)
2 Words in parentheses are optional – they may be put in or left out.
3 Words divided by a stroke (/) show possible variations.
4 Words *in italics* in this section are there purely as an example, to show how a phrase or structure is used in sentences.

12.1 ● Language problems

How to show you don't understand

bitte?	pardon?
ich verstehe nicht	I don't understand
ich habe das/dich nicht verstanden	I didn't understand that/you
ich verstehe nicht, was du meinst	I don't understand what you mean

How to ask for things to be repeated

bitte? / wie bitte?	pardon?
noch mal, bitte	once again, please

How to ask for things to be said more slowly

(etwas) langsamer, bitte!	(a bit) slower, please!
(bitte) nicht so schnell!	not so fast (please)!
könntest du bitte etwas langsamer sprechen?	could you please speak a bit more slowly?

How to find out the meaning of things and get the right word

was heißt das?	what does that mean?
was heißt „*schlank*"?	what does '*schlank*' mean?
„*eine Taschenlampe*"? Was ist das?	a '*Taschenlampe*'? What's that?
was/wie heißt das auf deutsch/englisch?	what's that in German/English?
wie sagt man . . .?	how do you say . . .?
ich habe das Wort vergessen	I've forgotten the word

How to check information

du heißt Peter, ja?	*you're called Peter,* aren't you?
das ist blöd, nicht (wahr)?	*that's stupid*, isn't it?
du hast „Ja" gesagt, oder?	*you said 'Yes'*, didn't you?
stimmt das?	is that right/correct/true?
ist das richtig?	is that correct?

How to check and give spellings

wie schreibt man das?	how do you spell that?
schreibt man das mit *D* oder *T*?	do you spell that with a *D* or a *T*?
Schmitt mit zwei *T*	*Schmitt* with two *T*s

(For more on the alphabet and spelling, see 11.1.)

How to say what you mean when you don't know the right word

das ist so etwas *aus Metall*	it's a sort of *metal* thing
ich brauche ein Dings (pl.: zwei Dinger)	I need a thingummy-jig
ich weiß nicht, wie man das sagt, aber *man schreibt damit*	I don't know how to say it but *you write with it*

How to correct yourself

Verzeihung!/Entschuldigung!	sorry!
nein, nicht „Heft" – „Hemd" (meine ich)	no, not 'Heft' – (I mean) 'Hemd'
nein, ich wollte sagen . . .	no, I wanted/meant to say . . .

12.2 • Dealing with people

[See also 12.3 Plans and intentions.]

How to greet people

guten Tag!	hello, good day, good afternoon
grüß Gott!	hello, etc. – in South Germany and Austria
guten Morgen!	good morning!
guten Abend!	good evening!
gute Nacht!	good night!
grüß dich, *Petra*!	hi, *Petra*! [informal]
hallo!	hi!

How to say goodbye

auf Wiedersehen/auf Wiederschauen!	goodbye!
auf Wiederhören!	goodbye! [on telephone]
tschüs!/tschüß!	bye! [informal]
bis *morgen*!	see you *tomorrow*!

How to wish people well

alles Gute!	all the best!
ich wünsche dir alles Gute!	I wish you all the best!
herzlichen Glückwunsch!	congratulations!
gratuliere!	congratulations!
ich gratuliere (dir) (zu + dat.)	congratulations (on . . .)
herzlichen Glückwunsch zum Geburtstag!	happy birthday!
guten Appetit!	enjoy your meal!
Mahlzeit!	enjoy your meal!
gute Besserung!	get well soon!
gute Reise!/gute Fahrt!	enjoy your journey!/have a good trip!
viel Spaß!	have a good time!
schlaf gut!	sleep well!
schönes Wochenende!	have a nice weekend!
schöne Ferien!	have a nice holiday!
frohe Weihnachten!	merry Christmas!
frohe Ostern!	happy Easter!
ein gutes neues Jahr!	have a happy new year!
prosit!/prost!/zum Wohl!	cheers!
prosit Neujahr!	here's to the new year!

How to reply to good wishes

danke!	thanks!
danke, gleichfalls!	thanks, the same to you!

How to send good wishes to other people

viele Grüße an *deinen Bruder*!	best wishes/love to *your brother*!
(einen) (schönen) Gruß an *Petra*!	best wishes/my regards to *Petra*!
grüß/grüßen Sie *Peter* von mir!	say hello to *Peter* for me/ give my regards to *Peter*

How to ask for things

ich möchte (bitte) (gern) . . .	I would like . . . (please)
kann ich bitte *ein Handtuch* haben?	may I have *a towel* please?
kann ich bitte *auf mein Zimmer gehen*?	may I *go up to my room*?
könnte ich bitte . . .?	please could I . . .?
ich habe/hätte eine Bitte	there's something I'd like to ask for

How to ask for help

hilfst du mir bitte?	will you help me please?
kannst du/könntest du . . .?	can you/could you . . .?
kannst du mir bitte helfen?	can you help me?
kannst du mir bitte *den Koffer tragen*?	can you please *carry my suitcase* for me?
kannst du mir bitte helfen, *den Sessel zu tragen*?	can you please help me to *carry the armchair*?
ich wäre sehr dankbar, wenn du mir helfen könntest	I'd be very grateful if you could help me
Hilfe!	help!

How to offer help

kann ich dir helfen?	can I help you?
was kann ich für dich tun?	what can I do for you?
kann ich (für dich) *abwaschen*?	can I *wash up* (for you)?
soll ich *die Tür aufmachen*?	shall I *open the door*?

How to thank people

danke (sehr/schön)	thank you (very much)
vielen Dank (für alles)	many thanks (for everything)
vielen Dank/danke für + acc.	thank you for . . .
danke, das ist/war sehr nett (von dir)	thanks, that is/was very nice (of you)
vielen Dank für deine Hilfe	thank you for your help

How to respond to thanks

bitte (schön/sehr)	don't mention it
gern geschehen	it's a pleasure [literally: gladly happened]
nichts zu danken	it was nothing [literally: nothing to thank]

How to enquire how people are   [See also 10.30d.]

wie geht's (dir)?	how are things/how are you?
gut, danke (und dir?)	fine, thanks (and you?)
auch gut, danke	I'm fine too, thanks
es geht mir ⎡gut / nicht so gut / schlecht⎤	I'm ⎡fine / not very well / not well⎤
wie geht's *deinem Bruder*?	how's *your brother*?
gut geschlafen?	did you sleep well?
schlaf gut! ['du' form]	sleep well!

How to apologise

(oh) Verzeihung!/Entschuldigung!	(oh) sorry!/pardon!
entschuldige! ['du' form]	sorry!/excuse me!
entschuldigen Sie!	sorry!/excuse me!
(es) tut mir leid	I'm sorry (about that)
es tut mir leid – das habe ich nicht gewollt	I'm sorry – I didn't mean to do that
es tut mir leid, aber . . ./daß . . .	I'm sorry but . . ./that . . .
leider *konnte ich nicht kommen*	unfortunately *I couldn't come*
das habe ich nicht so gemeint	I didn't mean it like that
das war ein Mißverständnis	it was a misunderstanding

How to make light of things

(das) macht (doch) nichts!	it doesn't matter!
das ist (doch) nicht (so) schlimm	it isn't (such) a tragedy
schon gut!	it's OK!
das kann passieren	it can easily happen
vergessen wir das!	let's forget (about) it!
das ist nicht meine/deine Schuld	it isn't my/your fault

How to agree

das stimmt!	that's right/true!
genau!/eben!	precisely!
das glaube/meine ich auch	that's what I think too
natürlich!	of course!
da hast du recht	you're right there
einverstanden!	agreed!

How to disagree

das stimmt nicht!	that isn't right/true!
bestimmt nicht	definitely not
das glaube ich nicht	I don't believe that
da hast du nicht recht	you're wrong there
doch!	yes! [contradicting someone's negative statement]

How to complain

was soll das?	what's going on?/what's that supposed to mean?
das geht (doch) nicht!	that isn't on!/ that's not possible!
ich finde das nicht gut	I think that's bad/ I don't agree with that
ich finde es nicht gut, daß . . .	I don't agree with the fact that . . .
so ein Mist!	how awful!
das ist doch blöd/Blödsinn/Quatsch!	that's stupid/rubbish/nonsense!

How to be unselfish

bitte (schön/sehr)!	here you are!/after you!
nach dir/Ihnen!	after you!
nimm du das doch!	you have it!/you take it!
stört es, wenn ich *das Radio anmache*?	will it bother/disturb you if I *turn the radio on*?

12.3 • Plans and intentions

How to make and ask for suggestions

gehen wir *ins Kino*! [the 'let's' form – see 10.10.e]	let's go *to the cinema*!
wollen wir *ins Kino gehen*?	shall we *go to the cinema*?
kommst du mit?	are you coming (with me/us)?
kommst du mit *ins Theater*?	are you coming (with me/us) *to the theatre*?
spielst du Tennis mit mir? (present tense question)	*will you play tennis with me*?
hast/hättest du Lust, *schwimmen* zu *gehen*?	do you feel like *going swimming*?
wie wär's (= wäre es) mit *einem Picknick*?	how about *a picnic*?
wie wär's, wenn wir *ins Kino gehen*?	how about *going to the cinema*?
ich möchte gern *fernsehen*	I'd like to *watch TV*
ich möchte lieber *Musik hören*	I'd rather *listen to music*
am liebsten möchte ich *Karten spielen*	most of all I'd like to *play cards*
was möchtest du machen?	what would you like to do?
wir könnten *in die Disko gehen*	we could *go to the disco*
ich habe eine Idee	I have an idea
ich schlage vor, wir *bleiben zu Hause*	I suggest we *stay at home*
was schlägst du vor?	what do you suggest?

How to talk about plans and intentions

ich gehe morgen einkaufen [present tense used with future meaning]	*I'm going shopping tomorrow*
ich werde *morgen einkaufen gehen* [future tense – see 10.29]	I shall *go shopping tomorrow*

ich $\begin{bmatrix} \text{möchte} \\ \text{will} \\ \text{soll} \\ \text{muß} \end{bmatrix}$ *morgen einkaufen gehen* [see modal verbs – 10.8] I $\begin{bmatrix} \text{would like to} \\ \text{want to} \\ \text{am to} \\ \text{have to} \end{bmatrix}$ go shopping tomorrow

was hast du *morgen* vor?	what have you got planned for *tomorrow?*
ich habe vor, *morgen einkaufen* zu *gehen*	I'm planning to *go shopping tomorrow*
ich habe beschlossen, *hier* zu *bleiben* [see 10.32.b]	I've decided to *stay here*
ich freue mich darauf	I'm looking forward to it
ich freue mich auf *die Fete*	I'm looking forward to *the party*
ich freue mich darauf, *nach Bonn* zu *fahren* [see 10.32.b]	I'm looking forward to *going to Bonn*
hast du *heute abend* Zeit/frei?	are you free *this evening?*

How to promise to do things

ich *mache das* [present tense]	I'll *do that*
ich *mache das* bestimmt/auf jeden Fall	I'll definitely *do that*
natürlich *mache ich das*	of course *I'll do that*
kein Problem!	no problem!
keine Angst! (ich mache das)	don't worry! (I'll do it)
abgemacht!	agreed!/that's settled!
das verspreche ich (dir)	I promise (you)

How to find out (or check) what you should do

was soll ich *machen?*	what shall I *do*/what am I supposed to *do?*
soll ich *den Tisch decken?*	shall I *lay the table?*
(bis) wann soll ich *zurücksein?*	when shall I *be back* (by)?
wo soll ich *sitzen?*	where shall I *sit?*
ich *sitze hier*, ja?	I *sit here*, do I?
darf/kann ich *hier sitzen?*	may/can I *sit here?*
muß ich *eine Karte kaufen?*	must I/do I have to *buy a ticket?*
geht das (so)?	is it all right (like this/that)?

mache ich das richtig?

wir sehen fern, ja? Oder hast du etwas dagegen?

stört es, wenn *ich fernsehe?*

am I doing it right?

we'll watch TV, shall we? Or don't you like the idea?

will it disturb/bother you if *I watch TV?*

How to tell people what to do and what not to do

komm doch mit!

nehmen Sie doch Platz!

mach das nicht!

hör auf!/laß das!

das ist verboten

das darfst du nicht machen

[See also 10.10 Commands and 12.2 How to ask for help.]

come with me/us!

have a seat!

don't do that

stop it!

that's not allowed

you mustn't do that

How to arrange times and places

wo/wann treffen wir uns?

wo/wann wollen wir uns treffen?

treffen wir uns *um acht*

treffen wir uns *um acht?*

treffen wir uns *vor dem Kino?*

sagen wir, *Viertel vor acht vor dem Kino*

etwas später/etwas früher

geht das?

einverstanden?

ist gut!/in Ordnung!

where/when shall we meet?

where/when shall we meet?

let's meet *at eight*

shall we meet *at eight?*

shall we meet *outside the cinema?*

let's say *quarter to eight outside the cinema*

a bit later/a bit earlier

is that all right?

agreed?

fine!/OK!

How to handle invitations and treats

ich möchte dich *zum Essen* einladen

hast/hätten du Lust, *morgen zum Essen* zu kommen?

danke für die Einladung

ich freue mich darauf

wann soll ich da sein?

ich lade dich ein!

danke für deine Gastfreundschaft

I'd like to invite you *to a meal*

do you fancy coming *for a meal tomorrow?*

thank you for the invitation

I look forward to it

when shall I be there?

I'm treating you! [= I'm paying for you]

thank you for your hospitality

119

How to hesitate about agreeing to something

ich weiß nicht	I don't know
das weiß ich noch nicht	I don't know yet
ich weiß noch nicht, *was ich morgen mache*	I don't know yet *what I'm doing tomorrow*
das kann ich noch nicht sagen	I can't say yet
das muß ich mir überlegen	I'll have to think about that
das/es kommt darauf an	it depends

How to refuse

nein, das kann ich nicht	no, I can't (do that)
nein, danke!	no thanks!
danke, das ist sehr nett, aber . . .	thank you, it's kind of you, but . . .
ich möchte gern, aber . . .	I'd like to, but . . .
es tut mir leid, aber . . .	I'm sorry, but . . .
vielleicht *später*	perhaps *later*

12.4 ● **Explaining**

● **Reporting**

How to describe people and things

[See also Adjectives, section 2.]

er/sie/es ist *alt*	he/she/it is *old*
sehr *alt*	very *old*
ziemlich *alt*	quite *old*
er ist/war *ein alter Mann*	*he* is/was *an old man*
er hat/hatte *blaue Augen*	*he* has/had *blue eyes*
es ist aus *Gold*	*it*'s made of *gold*
das ist/war *ein Mantel* mit *großen Knöpfen*	it is/was a *coat* with *big buttons*
das ist/war der Mann, der . . . [see 9.9 Relative clauses]	that is/was the man who . . .

How to say how to do things

man *schreibt die Adresse oben rechts*	you *write*/one *writes the address in the top right-hand corner*
du *machst es so* [see present tense 10.2–10.9]	you *do it like this*
dreh den Knopf nach rechts! [see commands 10.10]	*turn the knob to the right*

How to say what happened

[Use the perfect (Perfekt) or the simple past (Präteritum). See 10.12–10.27.]

How to report what people said

[Use reported speech. See 10.38.]

How to say what you know or are sure of

ich weiß, daß *die Bank heute geöffnet ist*	I know that *the bank is open today*
ich weiß, *wo Peter wohnt*	I know *where Peter lives*
ich bin sicher, daß . . .	I am sure that . . .
Petra fährt (ganz) bestimmt/sicher *mit*	*Petra will* definitely *come with us*
Petra fährt auf jeden Fall *mit*	*Petra* will definitely *come with us*
sicher!/bestimmt!/auf jeden Fall!	definitely!/certainly!

How to say what you do *not* know for sure

das weiß ich nicht genau/ ich bin nicht ganz sicher	I'm not quite sure
ich weiß nicht, *ob der Zug heute fährt*	I don't know *whether the train runs today*
ich bin nicht sicher, ob . . .	I'm not sure whether . . .
vielleicht	perhaps
vielleicht *fahren wir morgen nach Ulm*	perhaps *we'll go to Ulm tomorrow*
eventuell	possibly/perhaps
eventuell *fahren wir morgen nach Ulm*	perhaps *we'll go to Ulm tomorrow*
wahrscheinlich	probably
wahrscheinlich *kann man hier Geld wechseln*	you can probably change money here
es ist wohl *zu spät*	*it's* probably *too late*
es sieht so aus	that's the way it looks/ seems
es scheint so	that's the way it seems
es scheint, daß *Petra krank ist*	it seems as if/that *Petra's ill*
das kann sein	maybe/perhaps
es kann sein, *daß sie krank ist*	maybe *she's ill*

121

- **Your inclinations**

How to say what you like or dislike
[See also 10.30.b]

ACTIVITIES

ich *spiele* gern *Tennis*   I like *(playing) tennis*

PEOPLE AND GENERAL

ich habe *ihn/sie/es* gern   I like *him/her/it*
ich mag *ihn/sie/es* (gern)   I like *him/her/it*

FOODS

ich mag *Tomaten* (nicht gern)   I (don't) like *tomatoes*
ich esse (nicht) gern *Tomaten*   I (don't) like *tomatoes*

THINGS AND PLACES

dieses Buch gefällt mir (gut)   I like *this book* (very
                                                                    much)

diese Blumen gefallen mir (gut)   I like *these flowers* (very
                                                                    much)

es gefällt mir *hier*   I like it *here*
ich finde *das* sehr gut   I like *that* very much

How to say what you prefer
[See also 2.15 How to compare.]

ich *spiele* lieber *Tennis* (als *Federball*)   I prefer *(playing) tennis*
                                                                    (to *badminton*)

ich esse lieber *Äpfel* (als *Birnen*)   I prefer *apples* (to *pears*)
ich mag/habe *Peter* lieber (als *Hans*)   I prefer *Peter* (to *Hans*)
dieses Buch gefällt mir besser (als *das*)   I like *this book* better
                                                                    (than *that one*)

ich finde *Paris* besser als *Rom*   I prefer *Paris* to *Rome*

How to say what you like best
[See also 2.16 The superlative.]

am liebsten *spiele* ich *Fußball*   I like *(playing) football*
                                                                    best

ich mag/habe *Peter* am liebsten   I like *Peter* best
ich mag/esse *Tomaten* am liebsten   I like *tomatoes* best
dieses Buch gefällt mir am besten   I like *this book* best
ich finde *das* am besten   I like *this/that* best

How to say what you wish for or dream of

ich möchte (eines Tages) *Arzt/Ärztin werden*	I'd like to *become a doctor* (one day)
wenn es geht, möchte ich *nach Amerika fahren*	if possible I'd like to *go to America*
wenn ich *reich wäre*, würde ich . . .	if I *were rich* I would . . .
[See 10.39 Conditional sentences.]	

How to give your opinions

ich meine, daß *die „Cockroaches" eine sehr gute Band sind*	I think that *the 'Cockroaches' are a very good group*
ich glaube, daß . . .	I think/believe that . . .
ich finde, daß . . .	I think that . . .
meiner Meinung nach *ist das dumm*	in my opinion *that's stupid*
ich bin dafür	I'm in favour (of it)
ich bin dagegen	I'm against (it)
ich bin für + acc.	I'm in favour of . . .
ich bin gegen + acc.	I'm against . . .
was meinst du?	what do you think?

● **Feelings**

How to express pleasure and enthusiasm

toll!/prima!/Klasse! [informal]	great!
schön!	great!nice!
wie schön!	how nice!
das ist aber schön!	that's really nice!
das macht Spaß	it's fun
das hat (mir) Spaß gemacht	that was fun/I enjoyed that
ich bin (sehr) glücklich	I'm (very) happy
ich bin froh, daß *du da bist*	I'm glad that *you're here*
es freut mich, daß . . .	I'm glad that . . .
ich freue mich, daß . . .	I'm glad that . . .
das freut mich!	I'm glad (about that)!

How to express displeasure and horror

ach, nein!	oh no!
(das ist) schrecklich!/furchtbar!	(that's) horrible!/awful!
wie furchtbar!	how awful!
ich habe einen Schreck bekommen	I got a shock
ich bin/war (sehr) unglücklich/traurig	I am/was (very) unhappy/ sad

How to express anger

ich bin/war (sehr) böse	I am/was (very) angry/ annoyed
ich bin böse mit *ihm*	I'm angry with *him*
ich bin/war wütend	I am/was furious
das geht (doch) nicht!	that isn't on!

How to express astonishment

ach!	oh!
ach so!	I see!
nein!	no!
na sowas!	well I never!
das ist/war eine Überraschung	it is/was a surprise
komisch!	funny!/odd!
komisch, daß *Petra nicht da war*	it was odd that *Petra wasn't there*

How to express hopes

hoffentlich *kommt der Bus bald*	hopefully *the bus will come soon*
ich hoffe, *der Bus kommt bald*	I hope *the bus comes soon*
ich hoffe, daß *der Bus bald kommt*	I hope that *the bus comes soon*

How to express fears

hoffentlich *ist sie nicht krank*	I hope *she isn't ill*
ich habe Angst	I'm afraid
ich habe Angst, daß *sie krank ist*	I'm afraid that *she might be ill*
ich habe Angst vor *dem Zahnarzt*	I'm afraid of *the dentist*

How to express disappointment

schade!	pity!/shame!
wie schade!	what a pity/shame!
das ist aber schade	that's a pity/shame
(es ist) schade, daß *Hans krank ist*	it's a pity that *Hans is ill*
leider *mußten wir zu Hause bleiben*	unfortunately *we had to stay at home*
ich bin/war sehr enttäuscht (, daß) . . .	I am/was very disappointed (that . . .)

How to express relief

zum Glück *hatte ich genug Geld*	luckily *I had enough money*
glücklicherweise *konnte ich zahlen*	fortunately *I could pay*
ich bin/war (sehr) erleichtert	I am/was (very) relieved
endlich!	at last!
wir sind endlich *angekommen*	at last *we arrived*
endlich *sind wir angekommen*	at last *we arrived*

How to express indifference

das ist mir (ganz) egal	it's all the same to me
mir ist das (ganz) egal	it's all the same to me
das interessiert mich nicht	it doesn't interest me
meinetwegen	it's OK as far as I'm concerned

How to express boredom

das ist/war langweilig	it is/was boring
ich finde das langweilig	I find it boring
das ist/war nicht interessant	it is/was not interesting
ich langweile mich [see 10.7 Reflexive verbs]	I'm (getting) bored

How to express pain
[See 10.30 The dative used with verbs.]

au!	ow!/ouch!
das tut weh	it hurts
mein *Fuß* tut (mir) weh	my *foot*'s hurting (me)
ich habe *Magen*schmerzen	I've got *stomach*-ache

how to find it: index